NO FEAR SHAKESPEARE

A MIDSUMMER NIGHT'S DREAM

Edited by
John Crowther

SPARK
NOTES

EDITORIAL DIRECTOR: Justin Kestler

EXECUTIVE EDITOR: Ben Florman

DIRECTOR OF TECHNOLOGY: Tammy Hepps

SERIES EDITOR: John Crowther

CONTRIBUTING EDITORS: Anna Medvedovsky, Caolan Madden, Matt Blanchard

MANAGING EDITOR: Vincent Janoski

DESIGNER: Daniel Williams

This edition published by Spark Publishing

Spark Publishing
A Division of SparkNotes LLC
120 Fifth Avenue, 8th Floor
New York, NY 10011

03 04 05 06 07 **SN** 9 8 7 6 5 4 3 2 1

Please submit all comments and questions or report errors to *www.sparknotes.com/errors*

Library of Congress Cataloging-in-Publication Data available upon request

Printed and bound in the United States

ISBN 1-58663-848-3 (paperback)
ISBN 1-41140-048-8 (hardcover)

There's matter in these sighs, these profound heaves.
You must translate: 'tis fit we understand them.

(Hamlet, 4.1.1–2)

FEAR NOT.

Have you ever found yourself looking at a Shakespeare play, then down at the footnotes, then back at the play, and still not understanding? You know what the individual words mean, but they don't add up. SparkNotes' *No Fear Shakespeare* will help you break through all that. Put the pieces together with our easy-to-read translations. Soon you'll be reading Shakespeare's own words fearlessly—and actually enjoying it.

No Fear Shakespeare puts Shakespeare's language side-by-side with a facing-page translation into modern English—the kind of English people actually speak today. When Shakespeare's words make your head spin, our translation will help you sort out what's happening, who's saying what, and why.

A MIDSUMMER NIGHT'S DREAM

CHARACTERS

Theseus—The duke of Athens. Theseus is a hero from Greek mythology—he refers to the fact that he's Hercules' cousin at one point—so his presence signals to the reader that the play takes place in a mythical Greek past. At the beginning of the play, Theseus has recently returned from conquering the Amazons, a race of warrior women, and is about to marry the conquered Amazon queen, Hippolyta. Because of this impending wedding, the mood of the play is one of holiday festivity, characterized by a heightened sense of erotic expectation and anticipation. Theseus himself projects confidence, authority, and benevolent power.

Hippolyta—The legendary queen of the Amazons, engaged to marry Theseus. Although Hippolyta is marrying Theseus because he defeated her in combat, she does not act at all like an unwilling bride. Theseus is very courtly in his manner toward Hippolyta, and she is unfailingly deferential toward him.

Egeus—A respected nobleman in Theseus's court. Egeus complains to Theseus that his daughter, Hermia, refuses to marry Demetrius, Egeus's choice for her. Egeus's wish to control his daughter is quite severe—he asks Theseus to impose the death penalty on her if she refuses to marry Demetrius. Theseus, however, reduces the penalty for noncompliance from death to life as a nun.

Hermia—Egeus's daughter. Hermia is a beautiful young woman of Athens, and both Demetrius and Lysander are in love with her. Hermia defies her father's wish that she marry Demetrius because she is in love with Lysander. She is unusually strong-willed and independent—refusing to comply even when Theseus orders her to obey her father—and resolved to elope with Lysander. Hermia is also the childhood friend of Helena.

Lysander—A young nobleman of Athens in love with Hermia. Although Hermia's father refuses to let her marry Lysander, Lysander believes that love must conquer all obstacles, so he persuades Hermia to run away from her home and family with him, into the forest.

Demetrius—A young nobleman of Athens. In the past, Demetrius acted as if he loved Helena, but after Helena fell in love with him, he changed his mind and pursued Hermia. Emboldened by Egeus's approval of him, Demetrius is undeterred by the fact that Hermia does not want him.

Helena—A young woman of Athens in love with Demetrius. Helena has been rejected and abandoned by Demetrius, who had claimed to love her before he met her best friend, Hermia. Consequently, Helena tends to speak in a self-pitying tone. Moreover, she puts herself in dangerous and humiliating situations, running through the forest at night after Demetrius even though Demetrius wants nothing to do with her.

Robin Goodfellow—A "puck" or mischievous fairy who delights in playing pranks on mortals; he is sometimes referred to simply as Puck. Robin is Oberon's jester, and his antics are responsible for many of the complications that propel the play. At Oberon's bidding, Robin sprinkles "love juice" in the eyes of various characters to change who they love, but he makes mistakes in his application that create conflicts Oberon never intended. Though Robin claims to make these mistakes honestly, he enjoys the conflict and mayhem that his mistakes cause.

Oberon—The king of the fairies. Oberon begins the play at odds with his wife, Titania, because she refuses to relinquish control of a young Indian prince whom she has kidnapped, but whom Oberon wants for a knight. Oberon's desire for revenge on Titania leads him to send Robin to obtain the love-potion flower that creates so much of the play's confusion and farce.

Titania—The beautiful queen of the fairies. Titania resists the attempts of her husband, Oberon, to make a knight of the young Indian prince whom she has taken. Until Oberon gives up his demand, Titania has sworn to avoid his company and his bed. She is less upset by the fact that she and Oberon are apart than by the fact that Oberon has been disrupting her and her followers' magic fairy dances.

Nick Bottom—The overconfident weaver chosen to play Pyramus in a play that a group of craftsmen have decided to put on for Theseus's wedding celebration. Bottom is full of advice and self-confidence but frequently makes silly mistakes and misuses language. His simultaneous nonchalance about the beautiful Titania's sudden love for him and unawareness of the fact that Puck has transformed his head into that of an ass mark the pinnacle of his foolish arrogance.

Peter Quince—A carpenter and the nominal leader of the craftsmen's attempt to put on a play for Theseus's marriage celebration. Quince is often shoved aside by the abundantly confident Bottom. During the craftsmen's play, Quince plays the Prologue.

Francis Flute—The bellows-mender chosen to play Thisbe in the craftsmen's play for Theseus's marriage celebration. Forced to play a young girl in love, the bearded craftsman determines to speak his lines in a high, squeaky voice.

Robin Starveling—The tailor chosen to play Thisbe's mother in the craftsmen's play for Theseus's marriage celebration. Robin Starveling ends up playing the part of Moonshine.

Tom Snout—The tinker chosen to play Pyramus's father in the craftsmen's play for Theseus's marriage celebration. Tom Snout ends up playing the part of Wall, dividing the two lovers.

Snug—The joiner chosen to play the lion in the craftsmen's play for Theseus's marriage celebration. Snug worries that his roaring will frighten the ladies in the audience.

Philostrate—Theseus's Master of the Revels, responsible for organizing the entertainment for the duke's marriage celebration.

Peaseblossom, **Cobweb**, **Mote**, and **Mustardseed**—The fairies whom Titania orders to wait on Bottom after she falls in love with him.

NO FEAR SHAKESPEARE

A MIDSUMMER NIGHT'S DREAM

ACT ONE
SCENE 1

Enter THESEUS, HIPPOLYTA, *and* PHILOSTRATE, *with others*

THESEUS

Now, fair Hippolyta, our nuptial hour
Draws on apace. Four happy days bring in
Another moon. But oh, methinks how slow
This old moon wanes! She lingers my desires,
5   Like to a stepdame or a dowager
Long withering out a young man's revenue.

HIPPOLYTA

Four days will quickly steep themselves in night.
Four nights will quickly dream away the time.
And then the moon, like to a silver bow
10   New bent in heaven, shall behold the night
Of our solemnities.

THESEUS

               Go, Philostrate,
Stir up the Athenian youth to merriments.
Awake the pert and nimble spirit of mirth.
Turn melancholy forth to funerals.
15   The pale companion is not for our pomp.

Exit PHILOSTRATE

Hippolyta, I wooed thee with my sword
And won thy love doing thee injuries.
But I will wed thee in another key,
With pomp, with triumph, and with reveling.

Enter EGEUS *and his daughter* HERMIA, *and* LYSANDER *and*
DEMETRIUS

EGEUS

20   Happy be Theseus, our renownèd duke.

ACT ONE
SCENE 1

THESEUS and HIPPOLYTA enter with PHILOSTRATE and others.

THESEUS

Our wedding day is almost here, my beautiful Hippolyta. We'll be getting married in four days, on the day of the new moon. But it seems to me that the days are passing too slowly—the old moon is taking too long to fade away! That old, slow moon is keeping me from getting what I want, just like an old widow makes her stepson wait to get his inheritance.

HIPPOLYTA

No, you'll see, four days will quickly turn into four nights. And since we dream at night, time passes quickly then. Finally the new moon, curved like a silver bow in the sky, will look down on our wedding celebration.

THESEUS

Go, Philostrate, get the young people of Athens ready to celebrate and have a good time. Sadness is only appropriate for funerals. We don't want it at our festivities.

PHILOSTRATE exits.

Hippolyta, I wooed you with violence, using my sword, and got you to fall in love with me by injuring you. But I'll marry you under different circumstances—with extravagant festivals, public festivities, and celebration.

EGEUS enters with his daughter HERMIA, and LYSANDER and DEMETRIUS.

EGEUS

Long live Theseus, our famous and respected duke!

THESEUS
> Thanks, good Egeus. What's the news with thee?

EGEUS
> Full of vexation come I with complaint
> Against my child, my daughter Hermia.—
> Stand forth, Demetrius.—My noble lord,
25 > This man hath my consent to marry her.—
> Stand forth, Lysander.—And my gracious duke,
> This man hath bewitched the bosom of my child.—
> Thou, thou, Lysander, thou hast given her rhymes,
> And interchanged love tokens with my child.
30 > Thou hast by moonlight at her window sung
> With feigning voice verses of feigning love,
> And stol'n the impression of her fantasy
> With bracelets of thy hair, rings, gauds, conceits,
> Knacks, trifles, nosegays, sweetmeats—messengers
35 > Of strong prevailment in unhardened youth.
> With cunning hast thou filched my daughter's heart,
> Turned her obedience (which is due to me)
> To stubborn harshness.—And, my gracious duke,
> Be it so she will not here before your grace
40 > Consent to marry with Demetrius,
> I beg the ancient privilege of Athens.
> As she is mine, I may dispose of her—
> Which shall be either to this gentleman
> Or to her death—according to our law
45 > Immediately provided in that case.

THESEUS
> What say you, Hermia? Be advised, fair maid:
> To you your father should be as a god,
> One that composed your beauties, yea, and one
> To whom you are but as a form in wax,
50 > By him imprinted and within his power
> To leave the figure or disfigure it.
> Demetrius is a worthy gentleman.

THESEUS

Thanks, good Egeus. What's new with you?

EGEUS

I'm here, full of anger, to complain about my daughter Hermia.—Step forward, Demetrius.—My lord, this man, Demetrius, has my permission to marry her.—Step forward, Lysander.—But this other man, Lysander, has cast a magic spell over my child's heart.—You, you, Lysander, you've given her poems, and exchanged tokens of love with my daughter. You've pretended to be in love with her, singing fake love songs softly at her window by moonlight, and you've captured her imagination by giving her locks of your hair, rings, toys, trinkets, knickknacks, little presents, flowers, and candies—things that can really influence an impressionable young person. You've connived to steal my daughter's heart, making her stubborn and harsh instead of obedient (like she should be).—And, my gracious duke, if she won't agree to marry Demetrius right now, I ask you to let me exercise the right that all fathers have in Athens. Since she belongs to me, I can do what I want with her—as the law says: I can either make her marry Demetrius—or have her killed.

THESEUS

What do you have to say for yourself, Hermia? Think carefully, pretty girl. You should think of your father as a god, since he's the one who gave you your beauty. To him, you're like a figure that he's sculpted out of wax, and he has the power to keep that figure intact or to disfigure it. Demetrius is an admirable man.

HERMIA
So is Lysander.

THESEUS
                    In himself he is.
But in this kind, wanting your father's voice,
55   The other must be held the worthier.

HERMIA
I would my father looked but with my eyes.

THESEUS
Rather your eyes must with his judgment look.

HERMIA
I do entreat your grace to pardon me.
I know not by what power I am made bold
60   Nor how it may concern my modesty
In such a presence here to plead my thoughts,
But I beseech your grace that I may know
The worst that may befall me in this case,
If I refuse to wed Demetrius.

THESEUS
65   Either to die the death or to abjure
Forever the society of men.
Therefore, fair Hermia, question your desires.
Know of your youth. Examine well your blood—
Whether, if you yield not to your father's choice,
70   You can endure the livery of a nun,
For aye to be in shady cloister mewed,
To live a barren sister all your life,
Chanting faint hymns to the cold, fruitless moon.
Thrice-blessèd they that master so their blood
75   To undergo such maiden pilgrimage.
But earthlier happy is the rose distilled
Than that which, withering on the virgin thorn,
Grows, lives, and dies in single blessedness.

HERMIA

So is Lysander.

THESEUS

You're right, Lysander's admirable too. But since your father doesn't want him to marry you, you have to consider Demetrius to be the better man.

HERMIA

I wish my father could see them with my eyes.

THESEUS

No, you must see them as your father sees them.

HERMIA

Your grace, please forgive me. I don't know what makes me think I can say this, and I don't know if speaking my mind to such a powerful and noble person as yourself will damage my reputation for modesty. But please, tell me the worst thing that could happen to me if I refuse to marry Demetrius.

THESEUS

You'll either be executed or you'll never see another man again. So think carefully about what you want, beautiful Hermia. Consider how young you are, and question your feelings. Then decide whether you could stand to be a nun, wearing a priestess's habit and caged up in a cloister forever, living your entire life without a husband or children, weakly chanting hymns to the cold and virginal goddess of the moon. People who can restrain their passions and stay virgins forever are holy. But although a virgin priestess might be rewarded in heaven, a married woman is happier on Earth. A married woman is like a rose who is picked and made into a beautiful perfume, while a priestess just withers away on the stem.

HERMIA

> So will I grow, so live, so die, my lord,
80 > Ere I will my virgin patent up
> Unto his lordship, whose unwishèd yoke
> My soul consents not to give sovereignty.

THESEUS

> Take time to pause, and by the next new moon—
> The sealing day betwixt my love and me
85 > For everlasting bond of fellowship—
> Upon that day either prepare to die
> For disobedience to your father's will,
> Or else to wed Demetrius, as he would,
> Or on Diana's altar to protest
90 > For aye austerity and single life.

DEMETRIUS

> Relent, sweet Hermia—And, Lysander, yield
> Thy crazèd title to my certain right.

LYSANDER

> You have her father's love, Demetrius.
> Let me have Hermia's. Do you marry him.

EGEUS

95 > Scornful Lysander, true, he hath my love,
> And what is mine my love shall render him.
> And she is mine, and all my right of her
> I do estate unto Demetrius.

LYSANDER

> (to THESEUS) I am, my lord, as well derived as he,
100 > As well possessed. My love is more than his.
> My fortunes every way as fairly ranked,
> (If not with vantage) as Demetrius'.
> And—which is more than all these boasts can be—
> I am beloved of beauteous Hermia.
105 > Why should not I then prosecute my right?
> Demetrius, I'll avouch it to his head,
> Made love to Nedar's daughter, Helena,
> And won her soul. And she, sweet lady, dotes,

HERMIA

I'd rather wither away than give up my virginity to someone I don't love.

THESEUS

Take some time to think about this. By the time of the next new moon—the day when Hippolyta and I will be married—be ready either to be executed for disobeying your father, to marry Demetrius as your father wishes, or to take a vow to spend the rest of your life as a virgin priestess of the moon goddess.

DEMETRIUS

Please give in, sweet Hermia.—And Lysander, stop acting like she's yours. I've got more of a right to her than you do.

LYSANDER

Her father loves you, Demetrius. So why don't you marry him and let me have Hermia?

EGEUS

It's true, rude Lysander, I do love him. That's why I'm giving him my daughter. She's mine, and I'm giving her to Demetrius.

LYSANDER

(to THESEUS) My lord, I'm just as noble and rich as he is. I love Hermia more than he does. My prospects are as good as his, if not better. And beautiful Hermia loves me—which is more important than all those other things I'm bragging about. Why shouldn't I be able to marry her? Demetrius—and I'll say this to his face—courted Nedar's daughter, Helena, and made her fall in love with him. That sweet lady, Helena, loves devoutly. She adores this horrible and unfaithful man.

Devoutly dotes, dotes in idolatry
110   Upon this spotted and inconstant man.

THESEUS
I must confess that I have heard so much
And with Demetrius thought to have spoke thereof,
But being overfull of self-affairs,
My mind did lose it.—But, Demetrius, come.
115   And come, Egeus. You shall go with me.
I have some private schooling for you both.—
For you, fair Hermia, look you arm yourself
To fit your fancies to your father's will,
Or else the law of Athens yields you up
120   (Which by no means we may extenuate)
To death, or to a vow of single life.—
Come, my Hippolyta. What cheer, my love?—
Demetrius and Egeus, go along.
I must employ you in some business
125   Against our nuptial and confer with you
Of something nearly that concerns yourselves.

EGEUS
With duty and desire we follow you.

Exeunt. Manent LYSANDER *and* HERMIA

LYSANDER
How now, my love? Why is your cheek so pale?
How chance the roses there do fade so fast?

HERMIA
130   Belike for want of rain, which I could well
Beteem them from the tempest of my eyes.

LYSANDER
Ay me! For aught that I could ever read,
Could ever hear by tale or history,
The course of true love never did run smooth.
135   But either it was different in blood—

THESEUS

I have to admit I've heard something about that, and meant to ask Demetrius about it, but I was too busy with personal matters and it slipped my mind.—Anyway, Demetrius and Egeus, both of you, come with me. I want to say a few things to you in private.—As for you, beautiful Hermia, get ready to do what your father wants, because otherwise the law says that you must die or become a nun, and there's nothing I can do about that.—Come with me, Hippolyta. How are you, my love?—Demetrius and Egeus, come with us. I want you to do some things for our wedding, and I also want to discuss something that concerns you both.

EGEUS

We're following you not only because it is our duty, but also because we want to.

They all exit except LYSANDER *and* HERMIA.

LYSANDER

What's going on, my love? Why are you so pale? Why have your rosy cheeks faded so quickly?

HERMIA

Probably because my cheeks' roses needed rain, which I could easily give them with all the tears in my eyes.

LYSANDER

Oh, honey! Listen, in books they say that true love always faces obstacles. Either the lovers have different social standings—

HERMIA
O cross! Too high to be enthralled to low.

LYSANDER
Or else misgraffèd in respect of years—

HERMIA
O spite! Too old to be engaged to young.

LYSANDER
Or else it stood upon the choice of friends—

HERMIA
140   O hell, to choose love by another's eyes!

LYSANDER
Or, if there were a sympathy in choice,
War, death, or sickness did lay siege to it,
Making it momentary as a sound,
Swift as a shadow, short as any dream,
145   Brief as the lightning in the collied night;
That, in a spleen, unfolds both heaven and Earth,
And ere a man hath power to say "Behold!"
The jaws of darkness do devour it up.
So quick bright things come to confusion.

HERMIA
150   If then true lovers have been ever crossed,
It stands as an edict in destiny.
Then let us teach our trial patience,
Because it is a customary cross,
As due to love as thoughts and dreams and sighs,
155   Wishes and tears, poor fancy's followers.

LYSANDER
A good persuasion. Therefore, hear me, Hermia.
I have a widow aunt, a dowager
Of great revenue, and she hath no child.
From Athens is her house remote seven leagues,
160   And she respects me as her only son.
There, gentle Hermia, may I marry thee.
And to that place the sharp Athenian law
Cannot pursue us. If thou lovest me then,

HERMIA

Oh, what an obstacle that would be! Imagine being too high on the social ladder, and falling in love with someone beneath you.

LYSANDER

Or else they were very different ages—

HERMIA

How awful! Being too old to marry someone young.

LYSANDER

Or else their guardians and advisors said no—

HERMIA

What hell, to have your love life determined by someone else!

LYSANDER

Or, even if the lovers are a good match, their love might be ruined by war, death, or sickness, so that the affair only lasts an instant. Their time together might be as fleeting as a shadow or as short as a dream, lasting only as long as it takes a lightning bolt to flash across the sky. Before you can say "look," it's gone. That's how intense things like love are quickly destroyed.

HERMIA

If true lovers are always thwarted, then it must be a rule of fate. So let's try to be patient as we deal with our problem. It's as normal a part of love as dreams, sighs, wishes, and tears.

LYSANDER

That's the right attitude. So, listen, Hermia. I have an aunt who is a widow, who's very rich and doesn't have any children. She lives about twenty miles from Athens, and she thinks of me as a son. I could marry you there, gentle Hermia, where the strict laws of Athens can't touch us. So here's the plan. If you love me, sneak

Steal forth thy father's house tomorrow night.
165 And in the wood, a league without the town—
Where I did meet thee once with Helena
To do observance to a morn of May—
There will I stay for thee.

HERMIA
My good Lysander!
I swear to thee by Cupid's strongest bow,
170 By his best arrow with the golden head,
By the simplicity of Venus' doves,
By that which knitteth souls and prospers loves,
And by that fire which burned the Carthage queen
When the false Troyan under sail was seen,
175 By all the vows that ever men have broke
(In number more than ever women spoke),
In that same place thou hast appointed me,
Tomorrow truly will I meet with thee.

LYSANDER
Keep promise, love. Look, here comes Helena.

Enter HELENA

HERMIA
180 Godspeed, fair Helena! Whither away?

HELENA
Call you me "fair"? That "fair" again unsay.
Demetrius loves your fair. O happy fair!
Your eyes are lodestars, and your tongue's sweet air
More tunable than lark to shepherd's ear
185 When wheat is green, when hawthorn buds appear.
Sickness is catching. Oh, were favor so,
Yours would I catch, fair Hermia, ere I go.
My ear should catch your voice. My eye, your eye.
My tongue should catch your tongue's sweet melody.
190 Were the world mine, Demetrius being bated,
The rest I'd give to be to you translated.

out of your father's house tomorrow night and meet me in the forest a few miles outside of town. You remember the place—I met you there once with Helena to celebrate May Day.—I'll wait for you there.

HERMIA

Oh, Lysander, I swear I'll be there tomorrow. I swear by Cupid's strongest bow and his best gold-tipped arrow, by the Goddess of Love's innocent doves, by everything that ties lovers together, by the bonfire where Queen Dido burned herself to death when her lover Aeneas jilted her, and by all the promises that men have broken (and men have broken more promises than women have ever made). I give you my word, I will meet you at that spot tomorrow.

LYSANDER

Keep your promise, my love. Look, here comes Helena.

HELENA *enters.*

HERMIA

Hello, beautiful Helena! Where are you going?

HELENA

Did you just call me "beautiful"? Take it back. You're the beautiful one as far as Demetrius is concerned. Oh, you're so lucky! Your eyes are like stars, and your voice is more musical than a lark's song is to a shepherd in the springtime. Sickness is contagious—I wish beauty were contagious too! I would catch your good looks before I left. My ear would be infected by your voice, my eye by your eye, and my tongue would come down with a bad case of your melodious speech. If the world were mine, I'd give it all up—everything except Demetrius—to be you. Oh, teach me how you look

O, teach me how you look and with what art
You sway the motion of Demetrius' heart.

HERMIA
I frown upon him, yet he loves me still.

HELENA
195   Oh, that your frowns would teach my smiles such skill!

HERMIA
I give him curses, yet he gives me love.

HELENA
Oh, that my prayers could such affection move!

HERMIA
The more I hate, the more he follows me.

HELENA
The more I love, the more he hateth me.

HERMIA
200   His folly, Helena, is no fault of mine.

HELENA
None, but your beauty. Would that fault were mine!

HERMIA
Take comfort. He no more shall see my face.
Lysander and myself will fly this place.
Before the time I did Lysander see
205   Seemed Athens as a paradise to me.
Oh, then, what graces in my love do dwell,
That he hath turned a heaven unto a hell!

LYSANDER
Helen, to you our minds we will unfold.
Tomorrow night when Phoebe doth behold
210   Her silver visage in the watery glass,
Decking with liquid pearl the bladed grass
(A time that lovers' flights doth still conceal),
Through Athens' gates have we devised to steal.

HERMIA
(to HELENA*)* And in the wood where often you and I
215   Upon faint primrose beds were wont to lie,
Emptying our bosoms of their counsel sweet,

the way you do, and which tricks you used to make Demetrius fall in love with you.

HERMIA

I frown at him, but he still loves me.

HELENA

Oh, if only my smiles could inspire love as effectively as your frowns!

HERMIA

I curse him, but he loves me.

HELENA

If only my prayers could inspire that kind of affection!

HERMIA

The more I hate him, the more he follows me around.

HELENA

The more I love him, the more he hates me.

HERMIA

It's not my fault he acts like that, Helena.

HELENA

That's true, it's your beauty's fault. I wish I had a fault like that!

HERMIA

Don't worry. He won't see my face ever again. Lysander and I are running away from here. Before I saw Lysander, Athens seemed like paradise to me. But Lysander's so attractive that he's turned heaven into hell!

LYSANDER

Helena, we'll tell you about our secret plan. Tomorrow night, when the moon shines on the water and decorates the grass with tiny beads of pearly light (the time of night that always hides runaway lovers), we plan to sneak out of Athens.

HERMIA

(to HELENA) In the woods where you and I used to lounge around on the pale primroses, telling each other sweet secrets—that's where Lysander and I will

There my Lysander and myself shall meet.
And thence from Athens turn away our eyes
To seek new friends and stranger companies.
220   Farewell, sweet playfellow. Pray thou for us.
And good luck grant thee thy Demetrius!—
Keep word, Lysander. We must starve our sight
From lovers' food till morrow deep midnight.

LYSANDER
I will, my Hermia.

Exit **HERMIA**

Helena, adieu.
225   As you on him, Demetrius dote on you!

Exit **LYSANDER**

HELENA
How happy some o'er other some can be!
Through Athens I am thought as fair as she.
But what of that? Demetrius thinks not so.
He will not know what all but he do know.
230   And as he errs, doting on Hermia's eyes,
So I, admiring of his qualities.
Things base and vile, holding no quantity,
Love can transpose to form and dignity.
Love looks not with the eyes but with the mind.
235   And therefore is winged Cupid painted blind.
Nor hath Love's mind of any judgment taste—
Wings and no eyes figure unheedy haste.
And therefore is Love said to be a child,
Because in choice he is so oft beguiled.
240   As waggish boys in game themselves forswear,
So the boy Love is perjured everywhere.
For ere Demetrius looked on Hermia's eyne,
He hailed down oaths that he was only mine.
And when this hail some heat from Hermia felt,

meet. From then on we'll turn our backs on Athens. We'll look for new friends and keep the company of strangers. Goodbye, old friend. Pray for us, and I hope you win over Demetrius!—Keep your promise, Lysander. We need to stay away from each other until midnight tomorrow.

LYSANDER

I will, my Hermia.

HERMIA exits.

Goodbye, Helena. I hope Demetrius comes to love you as much as you love him!

LYSANDER exits.

HELENA

It's amazing how much happier some people are than others! People throughout Athens think I'm as beautiful as Hermia. But so what? Demetrius doesn't think so, and that's all that matters. He refuses to admit what everyone else knows. But even though he's making a mistake by obsessing over Hermia so much, I'm also making a mistake, since I obsess over him. Love can make worthless things beautiful. When we're in love, we don't see with our eyes but with our minds. That's why paintings of Cupid, the god of love, always show him as blind. And love doesn't have good judgment either—Cupid, has wings and no eyes, so he's bound to be reckless and hasty. That's why they say love is a child. because it makes such bad choices. Just as boys like to play games by telling lies, Cupid breaks his promises all the time. Before Demetrius ever saw Hermia, he showered me with promises and swore he'd be mine forever. But when he got all hot and

245 So he dissolved, and showers of oaths did melt.
     I will go tell him of fair Hermia's flight.
     Then to the wood will he tomorrow night
     Pursue her. And for this intelligence
     If I have thanks, it is a dear expense.
250 But herein mean I to enrich my pain,
     To have his sight thither and back again.

Exit

bothered over Hermia, his promises melted away. I'll go tell Demetrius that Hermia is running away tomorrow night. He'll run after her. If he's grateful to me for this information, it'll be worth my pain in helping him pursue my rival Hermia. At least I'll get to see him when he goes, and then again when he comes back.

HERMIA *exits.*

ACT 1, SCENE 2

Enter QUINCE *the carpenter, and* SNUG *the joiner, and*
BOTTOM *the weaver, and* FLUTE *the bellows-mender, and*
SNOUT *the tinker, and* STARVELING *the tailor*

QUINCE
Is all our company here?

BOTTOM
You were best to call them generally, man by man,
according to the scrip.

QUINCE
Here is the scroll of every man's name which is thought fit,
5   through all Athens, to play in our interlude before the duke
and the duchess, on his wedding day at night.

BOTTOM
First, good Peter Quince, say what the play treats on, then
read the names of the actors, and so grow to a point.

QUINCE
Marry, our play is The most lamentable comedy and most
10   *cruel death of Pyramus and Thisbe.*

BOTTOM
A very good piece of work, I assure you, and a merry.—
Now, good Peter Quince, call forth your actors by the
scroll.—Masters, spread yourselves.

QUINCE
Answer as I call you.—Nick Bottom, the weaver?

BOTTOM
15   Ready. Name what part I am for and proceed.

QUINCE
You, Nick Bottom, are set down for Pyramus.

ACT 1, SCENE 2

QUINCE, *the carpenter, enters with* SNUG, *the cabinetmaker;*
BOTTOM, *the weaver;* FLUTE, *the bellows-repairman;*
SNOUT, *the handyman; and* STARVELING, *the tailor.*

QUINCE

Is everyone here?

BOTTOM

Bottom means "individually," not "generally. Bottom frequently makes mistakes with words.

You should call their names generally, one person at a time, in the order in which their names appear on this piece of paper.

QUINCE

This is a list of the names of all the men in Athens who are good enough to act in the play we're going to perform for the duke and duchess on their wedding night.

BOTTOM

First, Peter Quince, tell us what the play is about, then read the names of the actors, and then shut up.

QUINCE

All right. Our play is called *A Very Tragic Comedy About the Horrible Deaths of Pyramus and Thisbe.*

BOTTOM

Let me tell you, it's a great piece of work, and very— funny.—Now, Peter Quince, call the names of the actors on the list. Men, gather around him.

QUINCE

Answer when I call your name.—Nick Bottom, the weaver?

BOTTOM

Here. Tell me which part I'm going to play, then go on.

QUINCE

You, Nick Bottom, have been cast as Pyramus.

BOTTOM
What is Pyramus? A lover or a tyrant?

QUINCE
A lover that kills himself, most gallant, for love.

BOTTOM
20 That will ask some tears in the true performing of it. If I do it, let the audience look to their eyes. I will move storms. I will condole in some measure.—To the rest.—Yet my chief humor is for a tyrant. I could play Ercles rarely, or a part to tear a cat in to make all split.

> *The raging rocks*
> 25 *And shivering shocks*
> *Shall break the locks*
> *Of prison gates.*
> *And Phoebus' car*
> *Shall shine from far*
> 30 *And make and mar*
> *The foolish Fates.*

This was lofty!—Now name the rest of the players.—This is Ercles' vein, a tyrant's vein. A lover is more condoling.

QUINCE
Francis Flute, the bellows-mender?

FLUTE
35 Here, Peter Quince.

QUINCE
Flute, you must take Thisbe on you.

BOTTOM

Medieval and Renaissance plays often featured tyrant characters— kings who gave long, ranting speeches.

What's Pyramus? A lover or a tyrant?

QUINCE

A lover who kills himself very nobly for love.

BOTTOM

I'll have to cry to make my performance believable. And as soon as I start crying, oh boy, the audience had better watch out, because they'll start crying too. I'll make tears pour out of their eyes like rainstorms. I'll moan very believably.—Name the other actors.—But I'm really in the mood to play a tyrant. I could do a great job with Hercules, or any other part that requires ranting and raving. I would rant and rave really well. Like this, listen.

> The raging rocks
> And shivering shocks
> Will break the locks
> Of prison gates.
> And the sun-god's car
> Will shine from far
> Away, and make and mar
> Foolish fate.

Oh, that was truly inspired!—Now tell us who the other actors are.—By the way, my performance just now was in the style of Hercules, the tyrant style. A lover would have to be weepier, of course.

QUINCE

Francis Flute, the bellows-repairman?

FLUTE

Here, Peter Quince.

QUINCE

Flute, you'll be playing the role of Thisbe.

FLUTE
What is Thisbe? A wandering knight?

QUINCE
It is the lady that Pyramus must love.

FLUTE
Nay, faith, let me not play a woman. I have a beard coming.

QUINCE
40 That's all one. You shall play it in a mask, and you may
speak as small as you will.

BOTTOM
An I may hide my face, let me play Thisbe too! I'll speak in
a monstrous little voice: "Thisne, Thisne!"—"Ah,
Pyramus, my lover dear, thy Thisbe dear and lady dear!"

QUINCE
45 No, no. You must play Pyramus.—And Flute, you Thisbe.

BOTTOM
Well, proceed.

QUINCE
Robin Starveling, the tailor?

STARVELING
Here, Peter Quince.

QUINCE
Robin Starveling, you must play Thisbe's mother.—Tom
50 Snout, the tinker?

SNOUT
Here, Peter Quince.

QUINCE
You, Pyramus' father.—Myself, Thisbe's father.—Snug
the joiner, you, the lion's part.—And I hope here is a play
fitted.

FLUTE

Who's Thisbe? A knight on a quest?

QUINCE

Thisbe is the lady Pyramus is in love with.

FLUTE

No, come on, don't make me play a woman. I'm growing a beard.

QUINCE

That doesn't matter. You'll wear a mask, and you can make your voice as high as you want to.

BOTTOM

In that case, if I can wear a mask, let me play Thisbe too! I'll be Pyramus first: "Thisne, Thisne!"—And then in falsetto: "Ah, Pyramus, my dear lover! I'm your dear Thisbe, your dear lady!"

QUINCE

No, no. Bottom, you're Pyramus.—And Flute, you're Thisbe.

BOTTOM

All right. Go on.

QUINCE

Robin Starveling, the tailor?

STARVELING

Here, Peter Quince.

QUINCE

Robin Starveling, you're going to play Thisbe's mother.—Tom Snout, the handyman.

SNOUT

Here, Peter Quince.

QUINCE

You'll be Pyramus's father—I'll play Thisbe's father myself—Snug, the cabinetmaker, you'll play the part of the lion.—So that's everyone. I hope this play is well cast now.

SNUG

55   Have you the lion's part written? Pray you, if it be, give it
     me, for I am slow of study.

QUINCE

     You may do it extempore, for it is nothing but roaring.

BOTTOM

     Let me play the lion too. I will roar, that I will do any man's
     heart good to hear me. I will roar, that I will make the duke
60   say, "Let him roar again. Let him roar again."

QUINCE

     An you should do it too terribly, you would fright the
     duchess and the ladies, that they would shriek. And that
     were enough to hang us all.

ALL

     That would hang us, every mother's son.

BOTTOM

65   I grant you, friends, if you should fright the ladies out of
     their wits, they would have no more discretion but to hang
     us. But I will aggravate my voice so that I will roar you as
     gently as any sucking dove. I will roar you an 'twere any
     nightingale.

QUINCE

70   You can play no part but Pyramus. For Pyramus is a sweet-
     faced man, a proper man as one shall see in a summer's day,
     a most lovely, gentlemanlike man. Therefore you must
     needs play Pyramus.

BOTTOM

     Well, I will undertake it. What beard were I best to play it
75   in?

QUINCE

     Why, what you will.

SNUG

Do you have the lion's part written down? If you do, please give it to me, because I need to start learning the lines. It takes me a long time to learn things.

QUINCE

You can improvise the whole thing. It's just roaring.

BOTTOM

Let me play the lion too. I'll roar so well that it'll be an inspiration to anyone who hears me. I'll roar so well that the duke will say, "Let him roar again. Let him roar again."

QUINCE

If you roar too ferociously, you'll scare the duchess and the other ladies and make them scream. And that would get us all executed.

ALL

Yeah, that would get every single one of us executed.

BOTTOM

Well, my friends, you've got to admit that if you scare the living daylights out of the ladies, they'd have no choice but to execute us. But I'll soften my voice—you know, aggravate it, so to speak—so that I'll roar as gently as a baby dove. I'll roar like a sweet, peaceful nightingale.

"Aggravate" is a mistake for "moderate."

QUINCE

You can't play any part except Pyramus. Because Pyramus is a good-looking man, the most handsome man that you could find on a summer's day, a lovely gentlemanly man. So you're the only one who could play Pyramus.

BOTTOM

Well then, I'll do it. What kind of beard should I wear for the part?

QUINCE

Whatever kind you want, I guess.

BOTTOM
> I will discharge it in either your straw-color beard, your
> orange-tawny beard, your purple-in-grain beard, or your
> French crown-color beard, your perfect yellow.

QUINCE
80
> Some of your French crowns have no hair at all, and then
> you will play barefaced.—But masters, here are your parts.
> And I am to entreat you, request you, and desire you to con
> them by tomorrow night and meet me in the palace wood,
> a mile without the town, by moonlight. There will we
85
> rehearse, for if we meet in the city we shall be dogged with
> company, and our devices known. In the meantime I will
> draw a bill of properties such as our play wants. I pray you,
> fail me not.

BOTTOM
> We will meet, and there we may rehearse most obscenely
90
> and courageously. Take pains. Be perfect. Adieu.

QUINCE
> At the duke's oak we meet.

BOTTOM
> Enough. Hold, or cut bowstrings.

Exeunt

BOTTOM

I'll play the part wearing either a straw-colored beard, or a sandy beard, or a red beard, or one of those bright yellow beards that's the color of a French coin.

QUINCE

Some French people don't have beards at all, because syphilis has made all their hair fall out, so you might have to play the part clean-shaven.—But gentlemen, here are your scripts, and I beg you to please learn them by tomorrow night. Meet me in the duke's forest a mile outside of town. It's best to rehearse there, because if we do it here in the city, we'll be bothered by crowds of people and everyone will know the plot of our play. Meanwhile, I'll make a list of props that we'll need for the play. Now make sure you show up, all of you. Don't leave me in the lurch.

BOTTOM

We'll be there, and there we'll rehearse courageously and wonderfully, truly obscenely. Work hard, know your lines. Goodbye.

QUINCE

We'll meet at the giant oak tree in the duke's forest.

BOTTOM

Got it? Be there, or don't show your face again.

They all exit.

ACT TWO
SCENE 1

Enter a FAIRY *at one side and* ROBIN (ROBIN GOODFELLOW) *at another*

ROBIN

How now, spirit? Whither wander you?

FAIRY

        Over hill, over dale,
        Thorough bush, thorough brier,
        Over park, over pale,
5   Thorough flood, thorough fire.
        I do wander everywhere
        Swifter than the moon's sphere.
        And I serve the fairy queen
        To dew her orbs upon the green.
10   The cowslips tall her pensioners be.
        In their gold coats spots you see.
        Those be rubies, fairy favors.
        In those freckles live their savors.
        I must go seek some dewdrops here
15   And hang a pearl in every cowslip's ear.
Farewell, thou lob of spirits. I'll be gone.
Our queen and all our elves come here anon.

ROBIN

The king doth keep his revels here tonight.
Take heed the queen come not within his sight.
20   For Oberon is passing fell and wrath
Because that she, as her attendant hath
A lovely boy stolen from an Indian king.
She never had so sweet a changeling.
And jealous Oberon would have the child
25   Knight of his train, to trace the forests wild.
But she perforce withholds the lovèd boy,
Crowns him with flowers, and makes him all her joy.

ACT TWO

SCENE 1

A FAIRY *and* ROBIN GOODFELLOW *(a "puck" or mischievous spirit) meet onstage.*

ROBIN

Hello, spirit! Where are you going?

FAIRY

I go over hills and valleys, through bushes and thorns, over parks and fenced-in spaces, through water and fire. I wander everywhere faster than the moon revolves around the Earth. I work for Titania, the Fairy Queen, and organize fairy dances for her in the grass. The cowslip flowers are her bodyguards. You'll see that their petals have spots on them—those are rubies, fairy gifts. Their sweet smells come from those little freckles. Now I have to go find some dewdrops and hang a pearl earring on every cowslip flower. Goodbye, you dumb old spirit. I've got to go. The queen and her elves will be here soon.

ROBIN

The king's having a party here tonight. Just make sure the queen doesn't come anywhere near him, because King Oberon is extremely angry. He's furious because she stole an adorable boy from an Indian king. She's never kidnapped such a darling human child before, and Oberon's jealous. He wants the child for himself, to accompany him on his wanderings through the wild forests. But the queen refuses to hand the boy over to Oberon. Instead, she puts flowers in the boy's hair and makes a fuss over him. And now Oberon and Titania refuse to speak to each other, or meet each

And now they never meet in grove or green,
By fountain clear or spangled starlight sheen.
30   But they do square, that all their elves for fear
Creep into acorn cups and hide them there.

FAIRY
Either I mistake your shape and making quite,
Or else you are that shrewd and knavish sprite
Called Robin Goodfellow. Are not you he
35   That frights the maidens of the villagery,
Skim milk, and sometimes labor in the quern
And bootless make the breathless housewife churn,
And sometime make the drink to bear no barm,
Mislead night-wanderers, laughing at their harm?
40   Those that "Hobgoblin" call you, and "sweet Puck,"
You do their work, and they shall have good luck.
Are not you he?

ROBIN
                    Thou speak'st aright.
I am that merry wanderer of the night.
I jest to Oberon and make him smile
45   When I a fat and bean-fed horse beguile,
Neighing in likeness of a filly foal.
And sometime lurk I in a gossip's bowl
In very likeness of a roasted crab,
And when she drinks, against her lips I bob
50   And on her withered dewlap pour the ale.
The wisest aunt telling the saddest tale
Sometime for three-foot stool mistaketh me.
Then slip I from her bum, down topples she,
And "Tailor!" cries, and falls into a cough,
55   And then the whole quire hold their hips and laugh,
And waxen in their mirth, and neeze, and swear
A merrier hour was never wasted there.
But, room, fairy! Here comes Oberon.

FAIRY
And here my mistress. Would that he were gone!

other anywhere—neither in the forest nor on the plain, nor by the river nor under the stars. They always argue, and the little fairies get so frightened that they hide in acorn cups and won't come out.

FAIRY

Unless I'm mistaken, you're that mischievous and naughty spirit named Robin Goodfellow. Aren't you the one who goes around scaring the maidens in the village, stealing the cream from the top of the milk, screwing up the flour mills, and frustrating housewives by keeping their milk from turning into butter? Aren't you the one who keeps beer from foaming up as it should, and causes people to get lost at night, while you laugh at them? Some people call you "Hobgoblin" and "sweet Puck," and you're nice to them. You do their work for them and give them good luck. That's you, right?

ROBIN

What you say is true. That's me you're talking about, the playful wanderer of the night. I tell jokes to Oberon and make him smile. I'll trick a fat, well-fed horse into thinking that I'm a young female horse. Sometimes I hide at the bottom of an old woman's drink disguised as an apple. When she takes a sip, I bob up against her lips and make her spill the drink all over her withered old neck. Sometimes a wise old woman with a sad story to tell tries to sit down on me, thinking I'm a three-legged stool. But I slip from underneath her and she falls down, crying, "Ow, my butt!" and starts coughing, and then everyone laughs and has fun. But step aside, fairy! Here comes Oberon.

FAIRY

And here's my mistress, Titania. I wish he'd go away!

Enter OBERON, *the King of Fairies, at one side with his train,
and* TITANIA, *the Queen, at the other, with hers*

OBERON

60   Ill met by moonlight, proud Titania.

TITANIA

What, jealous Oberon?—Fairies, skip hence.
I have forsworn his bed and company.

OBERON

Tarry, rash wanton. Am not I thy lord?

TITANIA

Then I must be thy lady. But I know
65   When thou hast stolen away from Fairyland,
And in the shape of Corin sat all day,
Playing on pipes of corn and versing love
To amorous Phillida. Why art thou here,
Come from the farthest step of India?
70   But that, forsooth, the bouncing Amazon,
Your buskined mistress and your warrior love,
To Theseus must be wedded, and you come
To give their bed joy and prosperity.

OBERON

How canst thou thus for shame, Titania,
75   Knowing I know thy love to Theseus? Glance at my credit
         with Hippolyta,
Didst thou not lead him through the glimmering night
From Perigouna, whom he ravishèd?
And make him with fair Ægles break his faith,
With Ariadne and Antiopa?

TITANIA

80   These are the forgeries of jealousy.
And never, since the middle summer's spring,
Met we on hill, in dale, forest, or mead,

OBERON, *the Fairy King, and his followers enter. On the opposite side of the stage,* TITANIA, *the Fairy Queen, and her followers enter.*

OBERON

How *not* nice to see you, Titania.

TITANIA

What, are you jealous, Oberon?—Fairies, let's get out of here. I've sworn I'll never sleep with him or talk to him again.

OBERON

Wait just a minute, you brazen hussy. Aren't you supposed to obey me, your lord and husband?

TITANIA

If you're my lord and husband, I must be your lady and wife, so you're supposed to be faithful to me. But I know for a fact that you snuck away from Fairyland disguised as a shepherd, and spent all day playing straw pipes and singing love poems to your new girlfriend. The only reason you left India was to come here and see that butch Amazon Hippolyta. She was your boot-wearing mistress and your warrior lover, and now that she's getting married to Theseus, you've come to celebrate their marriage.

OBERON

How can you stand there shamelessly talking about me and Hippolyta, when you know that I know about your love for Theseus? Weren't you the one who made him desert Perigouna in the middle of the night, right after he'd raped her? And weren't you the one who made him cheat on all of his other girlfriends, like Aegles, Ariadne, and Antiopa?

TITANIA

These are nothing but jealous lies. Since the beginning of midsummer, my fairies and I haven't been able to meet anywhere to do our dances in the wind without being disturbed by you and your arguments.

By pavèd fountain, or by rushy brook,
Or in the beachèd margent of the sea,
85   To dance our ringlets to the whistling wind,
But with thy brawls thou hast disturbed our sport.
Therefore the winds, piping to us in vain,
As in revenge, have sucked up from the sea
Contagious fogs, which falling in the land
90   Have every pelting river made so proud
That they have overborne their continents.
The ox hath therefore stretched his yoke in vain,
The ploughman lost his sweat, and the green corn
Hath rotted ere his youth attained a beard.
95   The fold stands empty in the drownèd field,
And crows are fatted with the murrain flock.
The nine-men's-morris is filled up with mud,
And the quaint mazes in the wanton green
For lack of tread are undistinguishable.
100   The human mortals want their winter here.
No night is now with hymn or carol blessed.
Therefore the moon, the governess of floods,
Pale in her anger, washes all the air,
That rheumatic diseases do abound.
105   And thorough this distemperature we see
The seasons alter: hoary-headed frosts
Fall in the fresh lap of the crimson rose,
And on old Hiems' thin and icy crown
An odorous chaplet of sweet summer buds
110   Is, as in mockery, set. The spring, the summer,
The childing autumn, angry winter change
Their wonted liveries, and the mazèd world,
By their increase, now knows not which is which.
And this same progeny of evils comes
115   From our debate, from our dissension.
We are their parents and original.

We haven't been able to meet on a hill or in a valley, in the forest or a meadow, by a pebbly fountain or a rushing stream, or on the beach by the ocean without you disturbing us. And because you interrupt us so that we can't dance for them, the winds have made fogs rise up out of the sea and fall down on the rivers so that the rivers flood, just to get revenge on you. So all the work that oxen and farmers have done in plowing the fields has been for nothing, because the unripe grain has rotted before it was ripe. Sheep pens are empty in the middle of the flooded fields, and the crows get fat from eating the dead bodies of infected sheep. All the fields where people usually play games are filled with mud, and you can't even see the elaborate mazes that people create in the grass, because no one walks in them anymore and they've all grown over. It's not winter here for the human mortals, so they're not protected by the holy hymns and carols that they sing in winter. So the pale, angry moon, who controls the tides, fills the air with diseases. As a consequence of this bad weather and these bad moods the seasons have started to change. Cold frosts spread over the red roses, and the icy winter wears a crown of sweet summer flowers as some sick joke. Spring, summer, fertile autumn and angry winter have all changed places, and now the confused world doesn't know which is which. And this is all because of our argument. We are responsible for this.

OBERON
Do you amend it then. It lies in you.
Why should Titania cross her Oberon?
I do but beg a little changeling boy,
120   To be my henchman.

TITANIA
                          Set your heart at rest.
The Fairyland buys not the child of me.
His mother was a votaress of my order,
And in the spicèd Indian air by night
Full often hath she gossiped by my side,
125   And sat with me on Neptune's yellow sands,
Marking th' embarkèd traders on the flood,
When we have laughed to see the sails conceive
And grow big-bellied with the wanton wind;
Which she, with pretty and with swimming gait
130   Following—her womb then rich with my young squire—
Would imitate, and sail upon the land
To fetch me trifles and return again
As from a voyage, rich with merchandise.
But she, being mortal, of that boy did die.
135   And for her sake do I rear up her boy,
And for her sake I will not part with him.

OBERON
How long within this wood intend you stay?

TITANIA
Perchance till after Theseus' wedding day.
If you will patiently dance in our round
140   And see our moonlight revels, go with us.
If not, shun me, and I will spare your haunts.

OBERON
Give me that boy and I will go with thee.

TITANIA
Not for thy fairy kingdom.—Fairies, away!
We shall chide downright, if I longer stay.
                          Exeunt TITANIA *and her train*

OBERON

Do something about it, then. You have the power to fix it. Why would Titania want to argue with her Oberon? All I'm asking for is to have that little human boy as part of my crew.

TITANIA

Get over it. I won't give up this child for all of Fairyland. His mother was one of my worshippers, and we always used to gossip together at night in India, sitting together by the ocean and watching the merchant ships sailing on the ocean. We used to laugh to see the sails fill up with wind so that they looked like they had big, pregnant bellies, as if the wind had gotten them pregnant. She would imitate them—since she was already pregnant with the little boy—and she would go sailing over the land herself to go get me little presents, and come back carrying gifts like she was a ship coming back from a voyage. But since she was a mortal, she died giving birth to that boy, and for her sake I'm raising him and will not give him up.

OBERON

How long do you plan to stay here in this forest?

TITANIA

Maybe until after Theseus's wedding day. If you behave yourself and join us in our circle dance and moonlight celebrations, then you can come with us. If not, leave me alone, and I'll stay away from your turf.

OBERON

Give me that boy and I'll come with you.

TITANIA

Not for your entire fairy kingdom.—Come, fairies, let's go. We're going to have an out-and-out brawl if I stay any longer.

TITANIA *and her* FAIRIES *exit.*

OBERON

145   Well, go thy way. Thou shalt not from this grove
        Till I torment thee for this injury.—*(to* ROBIN GOODFELLOW*)*
        My gentle Puck, come hither. Thou rememberest
        Since once I sat upon a promontory
        And heard a mermaid on a dolphin's back
150   Uttering such dulcet and harmonious breath
        That the rude sea grew civil at her song
        And certain stars shot madly from their spheres
        To hear the seamaid's music?

ROBIN

                           I remember.

OBERON

        That very time I saw (but thou couldst not)
155   Flying between the cold moon and the Earth,
        Cupid all armed. A certain aim he took
        At a fair vestal thronèd by the west,
        And loosed his love shaft smartly from his bow
        As it should pierce a hundred thousand hearts.
160   But I might see young Cupid's fiery shaft
        Quenched in the chaste beams of the watery moon,
        And the imperial votaress passèd on,
        In maiden meditation, fancy-free.
        Yet marked I where the bolt of Cupid fell.
165   It fell upon a little western flower,
        Before milk-white, now purple with love's wound.
        And maidens call it "love-in-idleness."
        Fetch me that flower. The herb I showed thee once.
        The juice of it on sleeping eyelids laid
170   Will make or man or woman madly dote
        Upon the next live creature that it sees.
        Fetch me this herb, and be thou here again
        Ere the leviathan can swim a league.

ROBIN

        I'll put a girdle round about the Earth
175   In forty minutes.

OBERON

Well, go on your way, then. You won't leave this grove until I've paid you back for this insult. *(to* ROBIN GOOD-FELLOW*)* My dear Puck, come here. You remember the time when I was sitting on a cliff, and I heard a mermaid sitting on a dolphin's back sing such a sweet and harmonious song that it calmed the stormy sea and made stars shoot out of the sky so they could hear her better?

ROBIN

Yes, I remember.

OBERON

That same night, I saw Cupid flying from the moon to the earth, with all of his arrows ready. (You couldn't see him, but I could.) He took aim at a beautiful young virgin who was sitting on a throne in the western part of the world, and he shot his arrow of love well enough to have pierced a hundred thousand hearts. But I could see that Cupid's fiery arrow was put out by watery, virginal moonbeams, so the royal virgin continued her virginal thoughts without being interrupted by thoughts of love. But I paid attention to where Cupid's arrow fell. It fell on a little western flower, which used to be white as milk but now has turned purple from being wounded by the arrow of love. Young girls call it "love-in-idleness." Bring me that flower. I showed it to you once. If its juice is put on someone's eyelids while they're asleep, that person will fall in love with the next living creature he or she sees. Bring me this plant, and get back here before the sea monster has time to swim three miles.

ROBIN

I could go around the world in forty minutes.

Exit ROBIN

OBERON

                        Having once this juice,
I'll watch Titania when she is asleep
And drop the liquor of it in her eyes.
The next thing then she waking looks upon—
Be it on lion, bear, or wolf, or bull,
180 On meddling monkey or on busy ape—
She shall pursue it with the soul of love.
And ere I take this charm from of her sight—
As I can take it with another herb—
I'll make her render up her page to me.
185 But who comes here? I am invisible.
And I will overhear their conference.

Enter DEMETRIUS, HELENA *following him*

DEMETRIUS
I love thee not, therefore pursue me not.
Where is Lysander and fair Hermia?
The one I'll stay, the other stayeth me.
190 Thou told'st me they were stol'n unto this wood.
And here am I, and wood within this wood,
Because I cannot meet my Hermia.
Hence, get thee gone, and follow me no more.

HELENA
You draw me, you hard-hearted adamant.
195 But yet you draw not iron, for my heart
Is true as steel. Leave you your power to draw,
And I shall have no power to follow you.

DEMETRIUS
Do I entice you? Do I speak you fair?
Or rather, do I not in plainest truth
200 Tell you I do not, nor I cannot, love you?

ROBIN *exits.*

OBERON

When I have the juice of that flower, I'll trickle some drops of it on Titania's eyes while she's sleeping. She'll fall madly in love with the first thing she sees when she wakes up—even if it's a lion, a bear, a wolf, a bull, a monkey, or an ape. And before I make her normal again—I can cure her by treating her with another plant—I'll make her give me that little boy as my page. But who's that coming this way? I'll make myself invisible and listen to their conversation.

DEMETRIUS *enters, followed by* HELENA.

DEMETRIUS

Look, I don't love you, so stop following me around. Where are Lysander and beautiful Hermia? Lysander I want to stop, but Hermia stops my heart from beating. You told me they escaped into this forest. And here I am, going crazy in the middle of the woods because I can't find my Hermia. Go away, get out of here, and stop following me.

HELENA

You attract me to you, you cruel magnet! But you must not attract iron, because my heart is as true as steel. If you let go of your power to attract me, I won't have any power to follow you.

DEMETRIUS

Do I ask you to follow me? Do I speak to you kindly? Don't I tell you in the clearest terms that I do not and cannot love you?

HELENA
　　And even for that do I love you the more.
　　I am your spaniel. And, Demetrius,
　　The more you beat me, I will fawn on you.
　　Use me but as your spaniel—spurn me, strike me,
205　Neglect me, lose me. Only give me leave,
　　Unworthy as I am, to follow you.
　　What worser place can I beg in your love—
　　And yet a place of high respect with me—
　　Than to be usèd as you use your dog?

DEMETRIUS
210　Tempt not too much the hatred of my spirit.
　　For I am sick when I do look on thee.

HELENA
　　And I am sick when I look not on you.

DEMETRIUS
　　You do impeach your modesty too much,
　　To leave the city and commit yourself
215　Into the hands of one that loves you not,
　　To trust the opportunity of night
　　And the ill counsel of a desert place
　　With the rich worth of your virginity.

HELENA
　　Your virtue is my privilege. For that
220　It is not night when I do see your face.
　　Therefore I think I am not in the night.
　　Nor doth this wood lack worlds of company,
　　For you in my respect are all the world.
　　Then how can it be said I am alone
225　When all the world is here to look on me?

DEMETRIUS
　　I'll run from thee and hide me in the brakes,
　　And leave thee to the mercy of wild beasts.

HELENA
　　The wildest hath not such a heart as you.
　　Run when you will, the story shall be changed.

HELENA

> Yes, but that makes me love you even more. I'm your little dog, Demetrius. The more you beat me, the more I'll love you. Treat me like you would treat a dog—kick me, hit me, neglect me, try to lose me. Just let me follow behind you, even though I'm not good enough for you. Could I ask for a worse place in your heart than to be treated as you would treat a dog? And yet I would consider it an honor to be your dog.

DEMETRIUS

> Don't push it. Just looking at you makes me sick.

HELENA

> And I get sick when I can't look at you.

DEMETRIUS

> You're risking your reputation by leaving the city and stalking someone who doesn't love you. Standing around alone in a deserted area in the middle of the night isn't the best way to protect your virginity.

HELENA

> I rely on your virtue to protect me. And because I can see your shining face, it doesn't feel like nighttime to me. This forest doesn't seem deserted when you're here, because you are all the world to me. So how can anyone say I'm alone, when the whole world is here to look at me?

DEMETRIUS

> I'll run away from you and hide in the bushes, and leave you to the mercy of wild animals.

HELENA

> The wildest animal isn't as cruel as you are. Run whenever you want to. The story of Daphne and Apollo will be changed: the lustful god Apollo runs

230 Apollo flies and Daphne holds the chase.
The dove pursues the griffin. The mild hind
Makes speed to catch the tiger—bootless speed,
When cowardice pursues and valor flies.

DEMETRIUS
I will not stay thy questions. Let me go.
235 Or if thou follow me, do not believe
But I shall do thee mischief in the wood.

HELENA
Ay, in the temple, in the town, the field
You do me mischief. Fie, Demetrius!
Your wrongs do set a scandal on my sex.
240 We cannot fight for love as men may do.
We should be wooed and were not made to woo.

Exit DEMETRIUS

I'll follow thee and make a heaven of hell,
To die upon the hand I love so well.

Exit HELENA

OBERON
Fare thee well, nymph. Ere he do leave this grove,
245 Thou shalt fly him and he shall seek thy love.

Enter ROBIN

Hast thou the flower there? Welcome, wanderer.

ROBIN
Ay, there it is.

OBERON
                    I pray thee, give it me.
(takes flower from ROBIN*)*
I know a bank where the wild thyme blows,
Where oxlips and the nodding violet grows,
250 Quite overcanopied with luscious woodbine,
With sweet musk roses and with eglantine.
There sleeps Titania sometime of the night,

away from the virginal nymph Daphne who pursues him, the dove chases after the griffin, which is usually its predator, and the gentle deer tries to hunt down the tiger—speed is useless when the cowardly person chases and the brave person runs away.

DEMETRIUS

I'm not sticking around to listen to you any longer. Leave me alone. Or if you follow me, you'd better understand that I'll do something bad to you in the forest.

HELENA

Yes, you already hurt me in the church, in the town, and in the fields. Shame on you, Demetrius! Your behavior is an insult to all women. We cannot fight for love as men can. We should be pursued and courted. We weren't made to do the pursuing.

DEMETRIUS *exits.*

I'll follow you and turn this hell I'm in into a kind of heaven. It would be heavenly to be killed by someone I love so much.

HELENA *exits.*

OBERON

Goodbye, nymph. Before he leaves this part of the forest, you'll change places: you'll be the one running away, and he'll be in love with you.

ROBIN *enters.*

Do you have the flower? Welcome, traveler.

ROBIN

Yes, here it is.

OBERON

Please, give it to me. *(he takes the flower from* ROBIN*)* I know a place where wild thyme blooms, and oxlips and violets grow. It's covered over with luscious hon-

Lulled in these flowers with dances and delight.
And there the snake throws her enameled skin,
255   Weed wide enough to wrap a fairy in.
And with the juice of this I'll streak her eyes
And make her full of hateful fantasies.
(gives ROBIN *some of the flower)*
Take thou some of it and seek through this grove:
A sweet Athenian lady is in love
260   With a disdainful youth. Anoint his eyes.
But do it when the next thing he espies
May be the lady. Thou shalt know the man
By the Athenian garments he hath on.
Effect it with some care, that he may prove
265   More fond on her than she upon her love.
And look thou meet me ere the first cock crow.

ROBIN
Fear not, my lord. Your servant shall do so.

Exeunt severally

eysuckle, sweet muskroses and sweetbrier. Titania sleeps there sometimes at night, lulled to sleep among the flowers by dances and other delights. Snakes shed their skin there, and the shed skin is wide enough to wrap a fairy in. I'll put the juice of this flower on Titania's eyes, and fill her with horrible delusions and desires. *(he gives* ROBIN *part of the flower)* You take some of it too, and look around in this part of the forest. A sweet Athenian lady is in love with a young man who wants nothing to do with her. Put some of this flower's juice on his eyes, and make sure to do it in such a way that the next thing he sees will be the lady. You'll be able to tell it's him because he's wearing Athenian clothes. Do it carefully, so that he'll end up loving her more than she loves him. And then make sure to meet me before the rooster's first crow at dawn.

ROBIN

Don't worry, sir. I'm at your service.

They all exit, separately.

ACT 2, SCENE 2

Enter TITANIA, *Queen of Fairies, with her train of* FAIRIES

TITANIA
Come now, a roundel and a fairy song.
Then for the third part of a minute, hence—
Some to kill cankers in the musk-rose buds,
Some war with reremice for their leathern wings
5   To make my small elves coats, and some keep back
The clamorous owl that nightly hoots and wonders
At our quaint spirits. Sing me now asleep.
Then to your offices and let me rest.

FAIRIES *sing*

FIRST FAIRY
(sings)
You spotted snakes with double tongue,
10   *Thorny hedgehogs, be not seen.*
Newts and blindworms, do no wrong.
Come not near our fairy queen.

FAIRIES
(sing)
Philomel, with melody
Sing in our sweet lullaby.
15   *Lulla, lulla, lullaby, lulla, lulla, lullaby.*
Never harm
Nor spell nor charm
Come our lovely lady nigh.
So good night, with lullaby.

FIRST FAIRY
(sings)
20   *Weaving spiders, come not here.*
Hence, you long-legged spinners, hence!

ACT 2, SCENE 2

TITANIA, *the Fairy Queen, enters with her following of*
FAIRIES.

TITANIA

Come, dance in a circle and sing a fairy song, and then
go off for a while to do your work. Some of you will kill
the worms infesting the rosebuds, some of you will
fight with bats to get their leathery wings, so we can
make coats for my small elves. Some of you will keep
that loud owl away, the one that hoots and wonders
every night at us dainty fairies. Sing me to sleep now,
and then go off to do your duties and let me rest.

The FAIRIES *sing.*

FIRST FAIRY

(singing)

> Snakes with forked tongues,
> And porcupines, don't be seen.
> Deadly lizards, don't be mean.
> Don't come near our fairy queen.

FAIRIES

(singing)

> Nightingale, melodiously
> Sing our sweet lullaby.
> Lulla, lulla, lullaby, lulla, lulla, lullaby.
> Let no harm
> Or spell or charm
> Come near our lovely lady.
> Say good night with a lullaby.

FIRST FAIRY

(singing)

> Spiders with your webs, stay away.
> You long-legged things, begone!

Beetles black, approach not near.
Worm nor snail, do no offense.

FAIRIES
(sing)

Philomel, with melody
25   *Sing in our sweet lullaby.*
Lulla, lulla, lullaby, lulla, lulla, lullaby.
Never harm
Nor spell nor charm
Come our lovely lady nigh.
30   *So good night, with lullaby.*

TITANIA *sleeps*

SECOND FAIRY
Hence, away! Now all is well.
One aloof stand sentinel.

Exeunt **FAIRIES**

Enter **OBERON**

OBERON
(squeezing flower juice on **TITANIA** *'s eyelids)*
What thou seest when thou dost wake,
Do it for thy true love take.
35   Love and languish for his sake.
Be it ounce or cat or bear,
Pard or boar with bristled hair,
In thy eye that shall appear,
When thou wakest, it is thy dear.
40   Wake when some vile thing is near.

Exit **OBERON**

Enter **LYSANDER** *and* **HERMIA**

LYSANDER
Fair love, you faint with wandering in the wood.
And to speak troth, I have forgot our way.

> *Black beetles, don't come near.*
> *Worms and snails, don't be bad.*

FAIRIES

> *(singing)*
>> *Nightingale, melodiously*
>> *Sing our sweet lullaby.*
>> *Lulla, lulla, lullaby, lulla, lulla, lullaby.*
>> *Let no harm*
>> *Or spell or charm*
>> *Come near our lovely lady.*
>> *Say good night with a lullaby.*

TITANIA *falls asleep.*

SECOND FAIRY

Okay, let's go! Everything's fine now. One of us will stay and stand guard.

The FAIRIES *exit.*

OBERON *enters.*

OBERON

(he squeezes flower juice on TITANIA*'s eyelids)*
Whatever you see first when you wake up, think of it as your true love. Love him and yearn for him, even if he's a lynx, a cat, a bear, a leopard, or a wild boar. Whatever's there when you wake up will be dear to you. Wake up when something nasty is nearby.

OBERON *exits.*

LYSANDER *and* HERMIA *enter.*

LYSANDER

My love, you look like you're about to faint from wandering in the woods for so long, and to tell you the truth, I've gotten us lost. We'll take a rest, if you think

We'll rest us, Hermia, if you think it good.
And tarry for the comfort of the day.

HERMIA

45   Be it so, Lysander. Find you out a bed,
For I upon this bank will rest my head.

LYSANDER

One turf shall serve as pillow for us both.
One heart, one bed, two bosoms, and one troth.

HERMIA

Nay, good Lysander. For my sake, my dear,
50   Lie further off yet. Do not lie so near.

LYSANDER

O, take the sense, sweet, of my innocence.
Love takes the meaning in love's conference.
I mean that my heart unto yours is knit
So that but one heart we can make of it.
55   Two bosoms interchainèd with an oath—
So then two bosoms and a single troth.
Then by your side no bed room me deny.
For, lying so, Hermia, I do not lie.

HERMIA

Lysander riddles very prettily.
60   Now much beshrew my manners and my pride
If Hermia meant to say Lysander lied.
But, gentle friend, for love and courtesy
Lie further off in human modesty.
Such separation as may well be said
65   Becomes a virtuous bachelor and a maid.
So far be distant. And, good night, sweet friend.
Thy love ne'er alter till thy sweet life end!

LYSANDER

Amen, amen to that fair prayer, say I.
And then end life when I end loyalty!
70   Here is my bed. Sleep give thee all his rest!

it's a good idea, and wait until daylight when things
will be easier.

HERMIA

Let's do that, Lysander. Find something to cushion
you while you sleep. I'm going to rest my head on this
little slope.

LYSANDER

We can both sleep together on the grass. We'll have
one heart, one bed, two bodies, and one faithful vow.

HERMIA

No, Lysander. Please, for my sake, sleep a little farther away. Don't sleep so close to me.

LYSANDER

Oh, sweetheart, I didn't mean anything naughty
when I said that. When lovers talk to each other, their
hearts should understand each other. I just meant that
our hearts are joined, so we can almost think of them
as one heart. Our two bodies are linked together by the
promises we've made to each other, so there are two
bodies and one faithful vow. So let me sleep next to
you. If I lie *next* to you, I won't lie *to* you—I'll be faithful and respect you.

HERMIA

Lysander's got a way with words. I would certainly be
rude and shameful if I had implied that you were a liar.
But please, darling, sleep a little farther away so we
can behave properly. It's only proper for a well-
behaved bachelor and a well-behaved girl to be phys-
ically separated like this. Stay away for now, and good
night, my sweet friend. I hope your love for me
remains this strong for your entire life!

LYSANDER

Amen to that. I hope my life ends before my loyalty to
you does. I'll sleep over here. Sleep well!

HERMIA
With half that wish the wisher's eyes be pressed!

HERMIA *and* LYSANDER *sleep*
Enter ROBIN

ROBIN
Through the forest have I gone.
But Athenian found I none,
On whose eyes I might approve
75   This flower's force in stirring love.
(sees LYSANDER *and* HERMIA*)*
Night and silence! Who is here?
Weeds of Athens he doth wear.
This is he, my master said,
Despisèd the Athenian maid.
80   And here the maiden, sleeping sound
On the dank and dirty ground.
Pretty soul! She durst not lie
Near this lack-love, this kill-courtesy.
(squeezes flower juice on LYSANDER*'s eyelids)*
Churl, upon thy eyes I throw
85   All the power this charm doth owe.
When thou wakest, let love forbid
Sleep his seat on thy eyelid.
So awake when I am gone,
For I must now to Oberon.

Exit ROBIN

Enter DEMETRIUS *and* HELENA, *running*

HELENA
90   Stay, though thou kill me, sweet Demetrius.
DEMETRIUS
I charge thee, hence, and do not haunt me thus.
HELENA
O, wilt thou darkling leave me? Do not so.

HERMIA

You sleep well too.

HERMIA *and* LYSANDER *sleep.* ROBIN *enters.*

ROBIN

I've been through the entire forest, but I haven't found any Athenian man to use the flower on. *(he sees* LYSANDER *and* HERMIA*)* Wait a second, who's this? He's wearing Athenian clothes. This must be the guy who rejected the Athenian girl. And here's the girl, sleeping soundly on the damp and dirty ground. Pretty girl! She shouldn't lie near this rude and heartless man. *(he puts flower juice on* LYSANDER*'s eyelids)* Jerk, I throw all the power of this magic charm on your eyes. When you wake up, let love keep you from going back to sleep. Wake up when I'm gone, because now I have to go to Oberon.

ROBIN *exits.*

DEMETRIUS *and* HELENA *enter, running.*

HELENA

Stop, Demetrius! Stop, even if only to kill me.

DEMETRIUS

I'm telling you, get out of here, and don't follow me around like this.

HELENA

Oh, will you leave me alone in the dark? Don't.

DEMETRIUS
    Stay, on thy peril. I alone will go.

                                        Exit DEMETRIUS

HELENA
    Oh, I am out of breath in this fond chase.
95 The more my prayer, the lesser is my grace.
    Happy is Hermia, wheresoe'er she lies,
    For she hath blessèd and attractive eyes.
    How came her eyes so bright? Not with salt tears.
    If so, my eyes are oftener washed than hers.
100 No, no, I am as ugly as a bear,
    For beasts that meet me run away for fear.
    Therefore no marvel though Demetrius
    Do, as a monster, fly my presence thus.
    What wicked and dissembling glass of mine
105 Made me compare with Hermia's sphery eyne?
    (sees LYSANDER*)* But who is here? Lysander, on the ground?
    Dead or asleep? I see no blood, no wound.—
    Lysander, if you live, good sir, awake.

LYSANDER
    (waking) And run through fire I will for thy sweet sake.
110 Transparent Helena! Nature shows art
    That through thy bosom makes me see thy heart.
    Where is Demetrius? Oh, how fit a word
    Is that vile name to perish on my sword!

HELENA
    Do not say so, Lysander. Say not so.
115 What though he love your Hermia? Lord, what though?
    Yet Hermia still loves you. Then be content.

LYSANDER
    Content with Hermia? No. I do repent
    The tedious minutes I with her have spent.
    Not Hermia but Helena I love.
120 Who will not change a raven for a dove?
    The will of man is by his reason swayed,

DEMETRIUS

Stay here at your own risk. I'm going on alone.

DEMETRIUS exits

HELENA

Oh, I'm out of breath from this foolish chase. The more I pray, the less I get out of it. Hermia is lucky, wherever she is, because she has beautiful eyes. How did her eyes get so bright? Not from crying. If that's the case, tears wash my eyes more than hers. No, no, I'm as ugly as a bear, since animals that see me run away in terror. So it's no surprise that Demetrius runs away from me as if I were a monster. What evil and deceitful mirror made me think I could rival Hermia's starry eyes? *(she sees* LYSANDER*)* But who's this here? Lysander, on the ground? Is he dead or sleeping? I don't see any blood or injuries—Lysander, if you're alive, wake up.

LYSANDER

(waking up) I'd even run through fire if you told me to. Radiant, beautiful Helena! I feel like Mother Nature has allowed me to see into your heart, as if by magic. Where is Demetrius? Oh, I'd kill that name with my sword if I could!

HELENA

Don't say that, Lysander. Don't say that. Why do you care that he loves Hermia? What does it matter? Hermia still loves you, so be happy.

LYSANDER

Happy with Hermia? No. I regret all the boring time I wasted with her. I don't love Hermia; I love Helena. Who wouldn't love a dove more than a crow? A man's desires are influenced by his logical mind, and it's

And reason says you are the worthier maid.
Things growing are not ripe until their season.
So I, being young, till now ripe not to reason.
125 And touching now the point of human skill,
Reason becomes the marshal to my will
And leads me to your eyes, where I o'erlook
Love's stories written in love's richest book.

HELENA
Wherefore was I to this keen mockery born?
130 When at your hands did I deserve this scorn?
Is 't not enough, is 't not enough, young man,
That I did never, no, nor never can,
Deserve a sweet look from Demetrius' eye,
But you must flout my insufficiency?
135 Good troth, you do me wrong, good sooth, you do,
In such disdainful manner me to woo.
But fare you well. Perforce I must confess
I thought you lord of more true gentleness.
Oh, that a lady of one man refused
140 Should of another therefore be abused!

Exit **HELENA**

LYSANDER
She sees not Hermia.—Hermia, sleep thou there.
And never mayst thou come Lysander near!
For as a surfeit of the sweetest things
The deepest loathing to the stomach brings,
145 Or as the heresies that men do leave
Are hated most of those they did deceive,
So thou, my surfeit and my heresy,
Of all be hated, but the most of me.—
And all my powers, address your love and might
150 To honor Helen and to be her knight.

Exit **LYSANDER**

simply logical that you're more worthy of love than Hermia is. Fruits and vegetables don't ripen until the right season of the year. Likewise, I'm young, and my sense of reason has just ripened. I can finally see the light. My logic has more control over my desires than it used to, and it's telling me to look into your eyes, where I see every love story ever told.

HELENA

Why does everyone always make fun of me? What have I done to deserve this kind of treatment from you? Is it not enough, is it not enough, young man, that I'll never be pretty enough to get a kind look from Demetrius? Do you have to harp on my inadequacy? My God, it's wrong for you to woo me in such a cruel, disdainful way. But goodbye. I have to tell you, I thought you were a much kinder person than this. Oh, how awful that a lady who's been rejected by one man should therefore be treated horribly by another one!

HELENA *exits.*

LYSANDER

She doesn't see Hermia—Hermia, keep sleeping, and don't come near me ever again! Eating too many sweets makes people sick to their stomachs, and people always hate the mistakes they made in the past worse than anyone else hates those mistakes. Hermia, you're the sweet I've had too much of, and the mistake I used to make, so I hate you more than anyone else does.—I'll use all my talents and efforts to serve Helen and bring her honor.

LYSANDER *exits.*

HERMIA
    (waking) Help me, Lysander, help me! Do thy best
    To pluck this crawling serpent from my breast.
    Ay me, for pity! What a dream was here.
    Lysander, look how I do quake with fear.
155   Methought a serpent eat my heart away,
    And you sat smiling at his cruel pray.
    Lysander!—What, removed?—Lysander, lord!—
    What, out of hearing, gone? No sound, no word?—
    Alack, where are you? Speak, an if you hear.
160   Speak, of all loves! I swoon almost with fear.
    No? Then I well perceive you all not nigh.
    Either death or you I'll find immediately.

Exit

ORIGINAL TEXT

HERMIA

(waking up) Help me, Lysander, help me! Get this snake off of my chest. Oh, my God! What a terrible dream I just had! Lysander, look how I'm shaking from fear. I thought a snake was eating my heart while you sat smiling and watching. Lysander!—What, is he gone?—Lysander, my lord!—What, is he out of earshot? Gone? No answer, nothing? Oh, God, where are you? Say something if you can hear me. Say something, please! I'm almost fainting with fear. Nothing? Then I guess you're nowhere nearby. I'll find you—or die—right away.

HERMIA *exits.*

ACT THREE

SCENE 1

TITANIA sleeps. Enter the clowns: BOTTOM, QUINCE, FLUTE,
SNUG, SNOUT, *and* STARVELING

BOTTOM
Are we all met?

QUINCE
Pat, pat. And here's a marvelous convenient place for our
rehearsal. This green plot shall be our stage, this hawthorn-
brake our tiring-house, and we will do it in action as we will
5   do it before the duke.

BOTTOM
Peter Quince—

QUINCE
What sayest thou, bully Bottom?

BOTTOM
There are things in this comedy of Pyramus and Thisbe
that will never please. First, Pyramus must draw a sword to
10   kill himself, which the ladies cannot abide. How answer
you that?

SNOUT
By 'r lakin, a parlous fear.

STARVELING
I believe we must leave the killing out, when all is done.

BOTTOM
Not a whit. I have a device to make all well. Write me a
15   prologue, and let the prologue seem to say we will do no
harm with our swords, and that Pyramus is not killed
indeed. And for the more better assurance, tell them that I,
Pyramus, am not Pyramus, but Bottom the weaver. This
will put them out of fear.

ACT THREE
SCENE 1

While TITANIA *is asleep onstage, the clowns—*BOTTOM, QUINCE, FLUTE, SNUG, SNOUT, *and* STARVELING*—enter.*

BOTTOM

Are we all here?

QUINCE

Right on time. This is the perfect place to rehearse. This clearing will be the stage, and this hawthorn bush will be our dressing room. Let's put on our play exactly as we'll perform it for the duke.

BOTTOM

Peter Quince—

QUINCE

What is it, jolly Bottom?

BOTTOM

There are things in this comedy of Pyramus and Thisbe that will never work. First of all, Pyramus has to take out a sword to kill himself, which the ladies in the audience won't be able to stand. What should we do about that?

SNOUT

By God, that's a real problem, it's true.

STARVELING

I think we'll have to leave out all the killing, come to think of it.

BOTTOM

Not at all! I've got a plan that will fix everything. Write me a prologue that I can recite to the audience before the play starts. I'll tell them that we won't hurt anyone with our swords, and that Pyramus isn't really dead. And to make it even clearer, we can tell them that I'm playing Pyramus but I'm not really Pyramus—really, I'm Bottom the weaver. That'll keep them from being afraid.

QUINCE
20   Well. We will have such a prologue, and it shall be written
        in eight and six.

BOTTOM
        No, make it two more. Let it be written in eight and eight.

SNOUT
        Will not the ladies be afeard of the lion?

STARVELING
        I fear it, I promise you.

BOTTOM
25   Masters, you ought to consider with yourselves. To bring
        in—God shield us!—a lion among ladies is a most dreadful
        thing. For there is not a more fearful wildfowl than your
        lion living. And we ought to look to 't.

SNOUT
        Therefore another prologue must tell he is not a lion.

BOTTOM
30   Nay, you must name his name, and half his face must be
        seen through the lion's neck. And he himself must speak
        through, saying thus—or to the same defect—"Ladies," or
        "Fair ladies," "I would wish you" or "I would request you"
        or "I would entreat you" "not to fear, not to tremble, my life
35   for yours. If you think I come hither as a lion, it were pity
        of my life. No, I am no such thing. I am a man as other men
        are." And there indeed let him name his name, and tell
        them plainly he is Snug the joiner.

QUINCE
        Well, it shall be so. But there is two hard things: that is, to
40   bring the moonlight into a chamber. For, you know,
        Pyramus and Thisbe meet by moonlight.

QUINCE

All right, we'll have a prologue then. We'll write it in alternating eight- and six-syllable lines, just like in a ballad.

BOTTOM

No, add a couple more syllables. Make it eight and eight.

SNOUT

Won't the ladies be scared of the lion?

STARVELING

I'm really worried about that.

BOTTOM

Sirs, you ought to think to yourself, bringing in—God forbid!—a lion amongst ladies is really terrible. There's no scarier wild bird than the living lion, and we should remember that.

SNOUT

So we need another prologue to tell everyone he's not a real lion.

BOTTOM

Bottom means to say "something to the same effect."

No, we can just announce the actor's name, and let his face show through the lion costume, and have him say something himself. He should say the following, or something else to the same defect—"Ladies," or "Lovely ladies," "I would like to ask you" or "I would like to request of you" or "I would like to beg you" "not to be afraid, and not to tremble with fear. I value your lives as highly as my own. If you thought I was a real lion, I would be risking my life. But no, I am not at all a lion. I am a man, just like other men." And then he should say his name, and tell them plainly that he's Snug the carpenter.

QUINCE

All right, that's what we'll do then. But there are two things we still have to figure out. How are we going to bring moonlight into a room? Because, you know, Pyramus and Thisbe meet by moonlight.

SNOUT
> Doth the moon shine that night we play our play?

BOTTOM
> A calendar, a calendar! Look in the almanac. Find out
> moonshine, find out moonshine!

QUINCE
45
> *(takes out a book)* Yes, it doth shine that night.

BOTTOM
> Why then, may you leave a casement of the great chamber
> window where we play open, and the moon may shine in at
> the casement.

QUINCE
> Ay. Or else one must come in with a bush of thorns and a
50
> lantern, and say he comes to disfigure, or to present, the
> person of Moonshine. Then, there is another thing: we
> must have a wall in the great chamber. For Pyramus and
> Thisbe, says the story, did talk through the chink of a wall.

SNOUT
> You can never bring in a wall. What say you, Bottom?

BOTTOM
55
> Some man or other must present Wall. And let him have
> some plaster, or some loam, or some roughcast about him
> to signify wall. And let him hold his fingers thus, and
> through that cranny shall Pyramus and Thisbe whisper.

QUINCE
> If that may be then all is well. Come, sit down, every
60
> mother's son, and rehearse your parts.—Pyramus, you
> begin. When you have spoken your speech, enter into that
> brake.—And so everyone according to his cue.

SNOUT

Will the moon be shining on the night we're performing our play?

BOTTOM

We need a calendar! Look in the almanac. Look up moonshine, look up moonshine!

QUINCE

(he takes out a book) Yes, the moon will shine that night.

BOTTOM

Well then, you can leave one of the windows open in the big hall where we'll be performing, and the moon can shine in through the window.

QUINCE

Yes, or else someone will have to come in carrying a bundle of sticks and a lantern and say he's come to disfigure, or represent, the character of Moonshine, because the man in the moon is supposed to carry sticks and a lantern. But there's still another problem: we need to have a wall in the big hall, because according to the story, Pyramus and Thisbe talked through a little hole in a wall.

Bottom means "figure" (symbolize), not disfigure.

SNOUT

You'll never be able to bring in a wall. What do you think, Bottom?

BOTTOM

Someone should play the part of Wall. He can have some plaster or clay or limestone or something on him to show the audience he's a wall. He can hold his fingers in a V-shape like this, and Pyramus and Thisbe can whisper to each other through that little crack.

QUINCE

If we can do that, everything will be all right. Now sit down, everybody, and rehearse your parts—Pyramus, you start. When you have said your lines, go hide in that bush.—Everyone else, go there too when you're not onstage.

Enter ROBIN *unseen*

ROBIN
    (aside) What hempen homespuns have we swaggering here,
    So near the cradle of the fairy queen?
65   What, a play toward? I'll be an auditor.
    An actor too, perhaps, if I see cause.

QUINCE
    Speak, Pyramus.—Thisbe, stand forth.

BOTTOM
    (as PYRAMUS*)* Thisbe, the flowers of odious savors sweet—

QUINCE
    "Odors," "odors."

BOTTOM
    (as PYRAMUS*)*

                    —odors savors sweet,
    So hath thy breath, my dearest Thisbe dear.
70   And by and by I will to thee appear. But hark, a voice!
        Stay thou but here awhile,

                              Exit BOTTOM

ROBIN
    (aside) A stranger Pyramus than e'er played here.

                                Exit ROBIN

FLUTE
    Must I speak now?

QUINCE
    Ay, marry, must you. For you must understand he goes but
    to see a noise that he heard, and is to come again.

FLUTE
75   *(as* THISBE*)* Most radiant Pyramus, most lily-white of hue,
    Of color like the red rose on triumphant brier,
    Most brisky juvenal and eke most lovely Jew,
    As true as truest horse that yet would never tire.
    I'll meet thee, Pyramus, at Ninny's tomb.

ROBIN *enters, unseen by the characters onstage.*

ROBIN

(to himself) Who are these country bumpkins swaggering around so close to where the fairy queen is sleeping? What? Are they about to put on a play? I'll watch. And I'll act in it, too, if I feel like it.

QUINCE

Speak, Pyramus.—Thisbe, come forward.

BOTTOM

(as PYRAMUS*)* Thisbe, flowers with sweet odious smells—

QUINCE

"Odors," "odors."

BOTTOM

(as PYRAMUS*)* —odors and smells are like your breath, my dearest Thisbe dear. But what's that, a voice! Wait here a while. I'll be right back!

BOTTOM *exits.*

ROBIN

(to himself) That's the strangest Pyramus I've ever seen.

ROBIN *exits.*

FLUTE

Am I supposed to talk now?

QUINCE

Yes, you are. You're supposed to show that you understand that Pyramus just went to check on a noise he heard and is coming right back.

FLUTE

(as THISBE*)* Most radiant Pyramus, you are as white as a lily, and the color of a red rose on a splendid rosebush, a very lively young man and also a lovely Jew. You are as reliable as a horse that never gets tired. I'll meet you, Pyramus, at Ninny's grave.

QUINCE

80   "Ninus' tomb," man. Why, you must not speak that yet.
        That you answer to Pyramus. You speak all your part at
        once, cues and all.—Pyramus, enter. Your cue is past. It is
        "never tire."

FLUTE

        Oh. (as thisbe) As true as truest horse that yet would never
85   tire.

        Enter **BOTTOM**, *with an ass's head, and* **ROBIN**

BOTTOM

        (as **PYRAMUS***)* If I were fair, Thisbe, I were only thine.

QUINCE

        Oh, monstrous! Oh, strange! We are haunted. Pray,
        masters! Fly, masters! Help!

        Exeunt **QUINCE**, **FLUTE**, **SNUG**, **SNOUT**, *and* **STARVELING**

ROBIN

        I'll follow you. I'll lead you about a round
90   Through bog, through bush, through brake, through brier.
        Sometime a horse I'll be, sometime a hound,
        A hog, a headless bear, sometime a fire.
        And neigh, and bark, and grunt, and roar, and burn,
        Like horse, hound, hog, bear, fire, at every turn.

        Exit **ROBIN**

BOTTOM

95   Why do they run away? This is a knavery of them to make
        me afeard.

        Enter **SNOUT**

QUINCE

That's "Ninus's grave," man. And don't say all of that yet. You're supposed to say some of it as a reply to Pyramus. You just said all your lines at once, cues and all.— Pyramus, enter. You missed your cue. It's "never get tired."

FLUTE

Oh! *(as* THISBE*)* As reliable as a horse that never gets tired.

ROBIN *enters with* BOTTOM, *with a donkey's head instead of a human head.*

BOTTOM

(as PYRAMUS*)* If I were handsome, my lovely Thisbe, I would still want only you.

QUINCE

Help! It's a monster! We're being haunted. Run, everyone, run!

QUINCE, FLUTE, SNUG, SNOUT, *and* STARVELING *exit.*

ROBIN

I'll follow you. I'll run you around in circles, through bogs and bushes and woods and thorns. Sometimes I'll take the shape of a horse, sometimes I'll take the shape of a hound or a pig or a headless bear. Sometimes I'll turn into fire! And I'll neigh like a horse and bark like a hound and grunt like a pig and roar like a bear and burn like a fire at every turn.

ROBIN *exits.*

BOTTOM

Why are they running away? This is some joke of theirs to scare me.

SNOUT *enters.*

SNOUT

O Bottom, thou art changed! What do I see on thee?

BOTTOM

What do you see? You see an ass head of your own, do you?

Exit SNOUT

Enter QUINCE

QUINCE

Bless thee, Bottom, bless thee. Thou art translated.

Exit QUINCE

BOTTOM

100   I see their knavery: this is to make an ass of me, to fright me
if they could. But I will not stir from this place, do what they
can. I will walk up and down here and I will sing, that they
shall hear I am not afraid.
(sings)

> *The ouzel cock, so black of hue*
105   > *With orange-tawny bill,*
> *The throstle with his note so true,*
> *The wren with little quill—*

TITANIA

(waking) What angel wakes me from my flowery bed?

BOTTOM

(sings)

> *The finch, the sparrow, and the lark,*
110   > *The plainsong cuckoo gray,*
> *Whose note full many a man doth mark*
> *And dares not answer "Nay"—*

SNOUT

Oh, Bottom, you've changed! What have you got on your head?

BOTTOM

What do you think I've got on my head? You're acting like an ass, don't you think?

SNOUT exits.

QUINCE enters.

QUINCE

God bless you, Bottom, God bless you. You've been changed. Reborn.

QUINCE exits.

BOTTOM

I see what they're up to. They want to make an ass of me, to scare me if they can. But I won't leave this spot, no matter what they do. I'll walk up and down and sing a song, so they'll know I'm not afraid.
(singing)
> The blackbird with its black feathers
> And its orange-and-tan beak,
> The thrush with its clear voice,
> The wren with its small, piping chirp—

TITANIA

(waking up) What angel is this who's waking me up from my bed of flowers?

BOTTOM

(singing)
> The finch, the sparrow, and the lark,
> The gray cuckoo with his simple song
> That many men hear
> But they don't dare say no to it—

For indeed, who would set his wit to so foolish a bird?
Who would give a bird the lie, though he cry "cuckoo"
115   never so?

TITANIA
I pray thee, gentle mortal, sing again.
Mine ear is much enamored of thy note.
So is mine eye enthrallèd to thy shape.
And thy fair virtue's force perforce doth move me
120   On the first view to say, to swear, I love thee.

BOTTOM
Methinks, mistress, you should have little reason for that.
And yet, to say the truth, reason and love keep little
company together nowadays. The more the pity that some
honest neighbors will not make them friends. Nay, I can
125   gleek upon occasion.

TITANIA
Thou art as wise as thou art beautiful.

BOTTOM
Not so, neither. But if I had wit enough to get out of this
wood, I have enough to serve mine own turn.

TITANIA
Out of this wood do not desire to go.
130   Thou shalt remain here whether thou wilt or no.
I am a spirit of no common rate.
The summer still doth tend upon my state.
And I do love thee. Therefore go with me.
I'll give thee fairies to attend on thee.
135   And they shall fetch thee jewels from the deep,
And sing while thou on pressèd flowers dost sleep.
And I will purge thy mortal grossness so
That thou shalt like an airy spirit go.—
Peaseblossom, Cobweb, Moth, and Mustardseed!

Of course they don't say "no"! Who'd waste his time talking to such a stupid bird? Who'd bother to accuse a bird of lying, even if the bird were telling him that his wife was cheating on him?

Cuckoos symbolize cuckolds (men whose wives cheat on them). The cuckoo's song was sometimes imagined as a mocking accusation that the men who hear it are cuckolds.

TITANIA

Please sing again, sweet human. I love to listen to your voice, and I love to look at your body. I know this is the first time I've ever seen you, but you're so wonderful that I can't help swearing to you that I love you.

BOTTOM

I don't think you've got much of a reason to love me. But to tell you the truth, reason and love have very little to do with each other these days. It's too bad some mutual friend of theirs doesn't introduce them. Ha, ha! No, I'm just kidding.

TITANIA

You're as wise as you are beautiful.

BOTTOM

No, that's not true. But if I were smart enough to get out of this forest, I'd be wise enough to satisfy myself.

TITANIA

Don't bother wishing you could leave this forest, because you're going to stay here whether you want to or not. I'm no ordinary fairy. I rule over the summer, and I love you. So come with me. I'll give you fairies as servants, and they'll bring you jewels from the depths of the ocean, and sing to you while you sleep on a bed of flowers. And I'll turn you into a spirit like us, so you won't die as humans do.—Come here, Pease-blossom, Cobweb, Moth, and Mustardseed!

Enter four fairies: PEASEBLOSSOM, COBWEB, MOTH, *and*
MUSTARDSEED

PEASEBLOSSOM
140   Ready.

COBWEB
                And I.

MOTH
                        And I.

MUSTARDSEED
                                And I.

ALL
        Where shall we go?

TITANIA
        Be kind and courteous to this gentleman.
        Hop in his walks and gambol in his eyes.
        Feed him with apricoks and dewberries,
145   With purple grapes, green figs, and mulberries.
        The honey bags steal from the humble-bees,
        And for night tapers crop their waxen thighs
        And light them at the fiery glowworms' eyes
        To have my love to bed and to arise.
150   And pluck the wings from painted butterflies
        To fan the moonbeams from his sleeping eyes.
        Nod to him, elves, and do him courtesies.

PEASEBLOSSOM
        Hail, mortal.

COBWEB
                Hail.

MOTH
                        Hail.

MUSTARDSEED
                                Hail.

BOTTOM
        I cry your worships' mercy, heartily.—I beseech your
155   worship's name.

NO FEAR SHAKESPEARE

*Four fairies—*PEASEBLOSSOM, COBWEB, MOTH, *and*
MUSTARDSEED*—enter.*

PEASEBLOSSOM
Ready.

COBWEB
Me too.

MOTH
Me too.

MUSTARDSEED
And me too.

ALL
Where should we go?

TITANIA
Be kind and polite to this gentleman. Follow him
around. Leap and dance for him. Feed him apricots
and blackberries, with purple grapes, green figs, and
mulberries. Steal honey from the bumblebees, and
make candles out of the bees' wax. Light them with
the light of glowworms, so my love will have light
when he goes to bed and wakes up. Pluck off colorful
butterfly wings, and use them to fan moonbeams away
from his eyes as he sleeps. Bow to him, fairies, and
curtsy to him.

PEASEBLOSSOM
Hello, mortal!

COBWEB
Hello!

MOTH
Hello!

MUSTARDSEED
Hello!

BOTTOM
I beg your pardon, sirs.—Please tell me your name,
sir?

COBWEB
Cobweb.

BOTTOM
I shall desire you of more acquaintance, good Master
Cobweb. If I cut my finger, I shall make bold with you.—
Your name, honest gentleman?

PEASEBLOSSOM
160   Peaseblossom.

BOTTOM
I pray you, commend me to Mistress Squash, your mother,
and to Master Peascod, your father. Good Master
Peaseblossom, I shall desire you of more acquaintance
too.— Your name, I beseech you, sir?

MUSTARDSEED
165   Mustardseed.

BOTTOM
Good Master Mustardseed, I know your patience well.
That same cowardly, giantlike ox-beef hath devoured
many a gentleman of your house. I promise you your
kindred hath made my eyes water ere now. I desire you of
170   more acquaintance, good Master Mustardseed.

TITANIA
Come, wait upon him. Lead him to my bower.
The moon methinks looks with a watery eye.
And when she weeps, weeps every little flower,
Lamenting some enforcèd chastity.
175   Tie up my love's tongue. Bring him silently.

Exeunt

COBWEB

Cobweb.

BOTTOM

I'd like to get to know you better, Mr. Cobweb. If I cut my finger, I'll use you as a bandage to stop the bleeding.—And your name, sir?

PEASEBLOSSOM

Peaseblossom.

BOTTOM

Please, give my regards to your mother, Mrs. Peapod, and your father, Mr. Peapod. Good Mr. Peaseblossom, I'd like to get to know you better too.—And you, may I ask what your name is, sir?

MUSTARDSEED

Mustardseed.

BOTTOM

Good Mr. Mustardseed, I know you very well. Those cowardly, gigantic sides of beef have been responsible for many of your family members getting eaten as a condiment on beef. I swear to you, many members of your mustard family have made my eyes water before. I look forward to getting to know you better, Mr. Mustardseed.

TITANIA

Take good care of him. Take him to my sleeping area. The moon looks sad to me. When she cries, all the little flowers cry too. They're sad because someone is prevented from having sex—or is having it against her will. Keep my lover quiet. Bring him to me in silence.

They all exit.

ACT 3, SCENE 2

Enter OBERON, *King of Fairies, solus*

OBERON
    I wonder if Titania be awaked.
    Then, what it was that next came in her eye,
    Which she must dote on in extremity.

Enter ROBIN

    Here comes my messenger.—How now, mad spirit?
5   What night-rule now about this haunted grove?

ROBIN
    My mistress with a monster is in love.
    Near to her close and consecrated bower,
    While she was in her dull and sleeping hour,
    A crew of patches, rude mechanicals
10   That work for bread upon Athenian stalls,
    Were met together to rehearse a play
    Intended for great Theseus' nuptial day.
    The shallowest thick-skin of that barren sort,
    Who Pyramus presented in their sport,
15   Forsook his scene and entered in a brake,
    When I did him at this advantage take,
    An ass's nole I fixèd on his head.
    Anon his Thisbe must be answerèd,
    And forth my mimic comes. When they him spy,
20   As wild geese that the creeping fowler eye,
    Or russet-pated choughs, many in sort,
    Rising and cawing at the gun's report,
    Sever themselves and madly sweep the sky—
    So at his sight away his fellows fly;
25   And, at our stamp, here o'er and o'er one falls.

ACT 3, SCENE 2

OBERON, *the Fairy King, enters.*

OBERON

I wonder if Titania is awake yet, and if she is, I wonder what the first thing she saw was. Whatever it is, she must be completely in love with it now.

ROBIN *enters.*

Ah, here comes my messenger.—What's going on, you crazy spirit? What havoc have you wreaked in this part of the forest?

ROBIN

My mistress Titania is in love with a monster. While she was sleeping in her bed of flowers, a group of bumbling idiots, rough workmen from Athens, got together nearby to rehearse some play they plan to perform on Theseus's wedding day. The stupidest one, who played Pyramus in their play, finished his scene and went to sit in the bushes to wait for his next cue. I took that opportunity to stick a donkey's head on him. When it was time for him to go back onstage and talk to his Thisbe, he came out of the bushes and everyone saw him. His friends ran away as fast as ducks scatter when they hear a hunter's gunshot. One of them was so frightened when he heard my footsteps that he yelled, "Murder!" and called for help from Athens. They were all so afraid that they completely lost their common sense. They started to become scared of inanimate objects, terrified by the thorns and briars that catch at their clothing and pull off their sleeves and hats. I led them on in this frightened, dis-

He "Murder!" cries and help from Athens calls.
Their sense thus weak, lost with their fears thus strong,
Made senseless things begin to do them wrong.
For briers and thorns at their apparel snatch,
30   Some sleeves, some hats—from yielders all things catch.
I led them on in this distracted fear
And left sweet Pyramus translated there.
When in that moment so it came to pass,
Titania waked and straightway loved an ass.

OBERON
35   This falls out better than I could devise.
But hast thou yet latched the Athenian's eyes
With the love juice, as I did bid thee do?

ROBIN
I took him sleeping—that is finished too—
And the Athenian woman by his side,
40   That, when he waked, of force she must be eyed.

Enter DEMETRIUS *and* HERMIA

OBERON
(aside to ROBIN*)* Stand close. This is the same Athenian.

ROBIN
(aside to OBERON*)* This is the woman, but not this the man.

DEMETRIUS
Oh, why rebuke you him that loves you so?
Lay breath so bitter on your bitter foe.

HERMIA
45   Now I but chide, but I should use thee worse.
For thou, I fear, hast given me cause to curse.
If thou hast slain Lysander in his sleep,
Being o'er shoes in blood, plunge in the deep,
And kill me too.

tracted state, and left sweet Pyramus there, transformed into someone with a donkey's head. At that exact moment, Titania woke up and immediately fell in love with him, an ass.

OBERON

This is going even better than I planned. But have you put the love juice from the flower on the eyes of that Athenian, as I asked you to do?

ROBIN

Yes, I found him when he was asleep—so that's taken care of too—and the Athenian woman was sleeping near him. When he woke up, he must have seen her.

DEMETRIUS *and* HERMIA *enter.*

OBERON

(speaking so that only ROBIN *can hear)* Step aside. Here's the Athenian coming now.

ROBIN

(speaking so that only OBERON *can hear)* That's definitely the woman I saw, but it's not the same man.

DEMETRIUS

Why are you so rude to someone who loves you so much? Save that kind of harsh language for your worst enemy.

HERMIA

I'm only scolding you now, but I should treat you much worse, because I'm afraid you've given me good reason to curse you. If you killed Lysander while he was sleeping, then you're already up to your ankles in blood. You might as well jump right into a bloodbath

50　The sun was not so true unto the day
　As he to me. Would he have stolen away
　From sleeping Hermia? I'll believe as soon
　This whole Earth may be bored, and that the moon
　May through the center creep and so displease
55　Her brother's noontide with th' Antipodes.
　It cannot be but thou hast murdered him.
　So should a murderer look, so dead, so grim.

DEMETRIUS
　So should the murdered look, and so should I,
　Pierced through the heart with your stern cruelty.
60　Yet you, the murderer, look as bright, as clear,
　As yonder Venus in her glimmering sphere.

HERMIA
　What's this to my Lysander? Where is he?
　Ah, good Demetrius, wilt thou give him me?

DEMETRIUS
　I had rather give his carcass to my hounds.

HERMIA
65　Out, dog! Out, cur! Thou drivest me past the bounds
　Of maiden's patience. Hast thou slain him then?
　Henceforth be never numbered among men!
　Oh, once tell true, tell true even for my sake—
　Durst thou have looked upon him being awake,
70　And hast thou killed him sleeping? O brave touch!
　Could not a worm, an adder, do so much?
　An adder did it, for with doubler tongue
　Than thine, thou serpent, never adder stung.

DEMETRIUS
　You spend your passion on a misprised mood.
75　I am not guilty of Lysander's blood.
　Nor is he dead, for aught that I can tell.

HERMIA
　I pray thee, tell me then that he is well.

DEMETRIUS
　An if I could, what should I get therefore?

and kill me, too. He was more faithful to me than the sun is to the daytime. Would he have snuck away from me while I was asleep? I'll believe that when I believe that there's a hole through the center of the earth, and the moon has passed all the way through to the other side. The only possibility is that you've murdered him. A murderer should look like you do, so pale and grim.

DEMETRIUS

That's how someone who's been murdered should look, and that's how I look. You've pierced me through the heart with your cruelty, and yet you, the murderer, look as bright and clear as a star in the sky.

HERMIA

What does that have to do with my Lysander? Where is he? Oh, good Demetrius, will you find him for me?

DEMETRIUS

I would rather feed his corpse to my dogs.

HERMIA

Get out, dog! You've driven me to my wit's end. Did you kill him, then? From now on I won't even consider you a human being. Oh, just tell the truth for once. tell the truth, if only for my sake.—Would you have even dared to look at him when he was awake? And did you kill him while he was sleeping? Oh, how brave of you! A snake could do that as easily as you could. A snake did do it, because no snake ever had a more forked, lying tongue than you have.

DEMETRIUS

You're getting all worked up over a misunderstanding. I didn't kill Lysander. ?As far as I know, he's not even dead.

HERMIA

Then please tell me he's all right.

DEMETRIUS

If I told you that, what would I get out of it?

HERMIA
A privilege never to see me more.
80   And from thy hated presence part I so.
See me no more, whether he be dead or no.

Exit HERMIA

DEMETRIUS
There is no following her in this fierce vein.
Here therefore for a while I will remain.
So sorrow's heaviness doth heavier grow
85   For debt that bankrupt sleep doth sorrow owe,
Which now in some slight measure it will pay,
If for his tender here I make some stay.
(lies down and sleeps)

OBERON
(to ROBIN*)* What hast thou done? Thou hast mistaken quite,
And laid the love juice on some true love's sight.
90   Of thy misprision must perforce ensue
Some true love turned, and not a false turned true.

ROBIN
Then fate o'errules that, one man holding troth,
A million fail, confounding oath on oath.

OBERON
About the wood go swifter than the wind,
95   And Helena of Athens look thou find—
All fancy-sick she is and pale of cheer,
With sighs of love, that costs the fresh blood dear.
By some illusion see thou bring her here.
I'll charm his eyes against she do appear.

ROBIN
100   I go, I go. Look how I go,
Swifter than arrow from the Tartar's bow.

Exit ROBIN

HERMIA

> The privilege of never seeing me again. And now I'm going to leave your despised company. You'll never see me again, whether or not he's dead.

> *HERMIA exits.*

DEMETRIUS

> I can't go after her when she's in a rage like this. So I'll stay here for a while. Sadness gets worse when you haven't had enough sleep. I'll try to sleep a little here. (*DEMETRIUS lies down and falls asleep*)

OBERON

> (*to ROBIN*) What have you done? You've made a mistake and put the love-juice on someone else, someone who was truly in love. Because of your mistake someone's true love must have turned bad, instead of this man's false love being turned into a true love.

ROBIN

> In that case, it must be fate. That's the way of the world. For every man who's faithful to his true love, a million end up running after a different lover.

OBERON

> Go around the forest, moving faster than the wind, and make sure you find Helena of Athens.—She's lovesick, and her face is pale from all the sighing she's been doing, because sighing is bad for the blood. Bring her here with some trick or illusion, and I'll put the charm on his eyes for when she comes.

ROBIN

> I go, I go, look at me go—faster than an arrow from a Tartar's bow.

The Tartars were a people from Asia Minor famous for their archery.

> *ROBIN exits*

OBERON
> *(squeezing flower juice into* DEMETRIUS*'s eyes)*
> Flower of this purple dye,
> Hit with Cupid's archery,
> Sink in apple of his eye.
105   When his love he doth espy,
> Let her shine as gloriously
> As the Venus of the sky.
> When thou wakest, if she be by,
> Beg of her for remedy.

Enter ROBIN

ROBIN
110   Captain of our fairy band,
> Helena is here at hand,
> And the youth, mistook by me,
> Pleading for a lover's fee.
> Shall we their fond pageant see?
115   Lord, what fools these mortals be!

OBERON
> Stand aside. The noise they make
> Will cause Demetrius to awake.

ROBIN
> Then will two at once woo one.
> That must needs be sport alone.
120   And those things do best please me
> That befall preposterously.

Enter LYSANDER *and* HELENA

LYSANDER
> Why should you think that I should woo in scorn?
> Scorn and derision never come in tears.
> Look, when I vow, I weep. And vows so born,
125   In their nativity all truth appears.

NO FEAR SHAKESPEARE

OBERON

(putting flower juice on DEMETRIUS's eyelids)
You purple flower, hit by Cupid's arrow, sink into the pupils of this man's eyes. When he sees the girl he should love, make her seem as bright to him as the evening star. Young man, when you wake up, if she's nearby, beg her to cure your lovesickness.

ROBIN *enters.*

ROBIN

Helena is nearby, boss. The young man who I mistook for this one is there too, begging her to love him. Should we watch this ridiculous scene? Lord, what fools these mortals are!

OBERON

Step aside. The noise they're making will wake up Demetrius.

ROBIN

Then the two of them will both pursue one girl. That will be funny enough, and preposterous situations are my favorite thing.

LYSANDER *and* HELENA *enter.*

LYSANDER

Why do you think I'm making fun of you when I tell you I love you? People don't cry when they're mocking someone. Look, when I swear that I love you, I cry, and when someone cries while he's making a promise, he's

How can these things in me seem scorn to you,
Bearing the badge of faith to prove them true?

HELENA
You do advance your cunning more and more.
When truth kills truth, O devilish holy fray!
130   These vows are Hermia's. Will you give her o'er?
Weigh oath with oath, and you will nothing weigh.
Your vows to her and me, put in two scales,
Will even weigh, and both as light as tales.

LYSANDER
I had no judgment when to her I swore.

HELENA
135   Nor none, in my mind, now you give her o'er.

LYSANDER
Demetrius loves her, and he loves not you.

DEMETRIUS
(waking) O Helena, goddess, nymph, perfect, divine!
To what, my love, shall I compare thine eyne?
Crystal is muddy. Oh, how ripe in show
140   Thy lips, those kissing cherries, tempting grow!
That pure congealèd white, high Taurus' snow,
Fanned with the eastern wind, turns to a crow
When thou hold'st up thy hand. Oh, let me kiss
This princess of pure white, this seal of bliss!

HELENA
145   O spite! O hell! I see you all are bent
To set against me for your merriment.
If you were civil and knew courtesy,
You would not do me thus much injury.
Can you not hate me, as I know you do,
150   But you must join in souls to mock me too?
If you were men, as men you are in show,
You would not use a gentle lady so

usually telling the truth. How can it seem like I'm making fun of you, when my tears prove that I'm sincere?

HELENA

You get trickier and trickier. You've made the same promises to me and to Hermia—they can't both be true! They must both be false. The promises you're making to me belong to Hermia. Will you abandon her? If you weighed the promises you made to me against the promises you made to her, they'd come out the same—they both weigh nothing. They're lies.

LYSANDER

I wasn't thinking clearly when I made those promises to her.

HELENA

And I don't believe you're thinking clearly now, as you break those promises.

LYSANDER

Demetrius loves her, and he doesn't love you.

DEMETRIUS

(waking up) Oh Helena, you goddess, you divine and perfect nymph! What can I compare your eyes to? Crystal isn't as clear as they are. Oh, your lips are as ripe as a pair of tempting cherries touching each other! The pure white of the snow on a mountaintop seems black as a crow's wing next to the whiteness of your hands. Oh, let me kiss your beautiful white hand. It'll make me so happy!

HELENA

Damn it! I see you're all determined to gang up on me for a few laughs. If you had any manners at all, you wouldn't treat me like this. Can't you just hate me, as I know you do? Do you have to get together to humiliate me too? If you were real men, as you pretend to be, you wouldn't treat a lady this way, making vows and promises and praising my beauty when I know you're really both disgusted by me. You're competing for

To vow, and swear, and superpraise my parts,
When I am sure you hate me with your hearts.
155 You both are rivals, and love Hermia,
And now both rivals to mock Helena—
A trim exploit, a manly enterprise,
To conjure tears up in a poor maid's eyes
With your derision! None of noble sort
160 Would so offend a virgin, and extort
A poor soul's patience, all to make you sport.

LYSANDER
You are unkind, Demetrius. Be not so.
For you love Hermia. This you know I know.
And here, with all good will, with all my heart,
165 In Hermia's love I yield you up my part.
And yours of Helena to me bequeath,
Whom I do love and will do till my death.

HELENA
Never did mockers waste more idle breath.

DEMETRIUS
Lysander, keep thy Hermia. I will none.
170 If e'er I loved her, all that love is gone.
My heart to her but as guest-wise sojourned,
And now to Helen is it home returned,
There to remain.

LYSANDER
Helen, it is not so.

DEMETRIUS
175 Disparage not the faith thou dost not know,
Lest to thy peril thou aby it dear.
Look, where thy love comes. Yonder is thy dear.

Enter HERMIA

HERMIA
Dark night, that from the eye his function takes,
The ear more quick of apprehension makes.

Hermia's love, and now you're competing to see which one of you can make fun of me the most. That's a great idea, a really manly thing to do—making a poor girl cry! No respectable person would offend an innocent girl just to have some fun.

LYSANDER

Don't be cruel, Demetrius. I know you love Hermia, and you know I know it. Right here, right now, I swear I'm giving up all my claims on her and handing her to you. In exchange, give up your claim to love Helena, since I love her and will love her until I die.

HELENA

Nobody's ever gone to so much trouble just to make fun of someone.

DEMETRIUS

Lysander, keep your Hermia. I don't want her. If I ever loved her, all that love is gone now. My love for her was temporary. Now I'll love Helena forever.

LYSANDER

Helena, it's not true.

DEMETRIUS

Don't insult a deep love that you don't understand, or you'll pay the price. Look, here comes the woman you love.

HERMIA *enters.*

HERMIA

It's hard to see clearly in the dark of night, but it's easier to hear well. I couldn't see you, Lysander, but I

180 Wherein it doth impair the seeing sense,
It pays the hearing double recompense.
Thou art not by mine eye, Lysander, found.
Mine ear, I thank it, brought me to thy sound
But why unkindly didst thou leave me so?

LYSANDER
185 Why should he stay, whom love doth press to go?

HERMIA
What love could press Lysander from my side?

LYSANDER
Lysander's love, that would not let him bide,
Fair Helena, who more engilds the night
Than all yon fiery oes and eyes of light.
190 Why seek'st thou me? Could not this make thee know
The hate I bear thee made me leave thee so?

HERMIA
You speak not as you think. It cannot be.

HELENA
Lo, she is one of this confederacy!
Now I perceive they have conjoined all three
195 To fashion this false sport, in spite of me.—
Injurious Hermia! Most ungrateful maid!
Have you conspired, have you with these contrived
To bait me with this foul derision?
Is all the counsel that we two have shared,
200 The sisters' vows, the hours that we have spent
When we have chid the hasty-footed time
For parting us—oh, is it all forgot?
All schooldays' friendship, childhood innocence?
We, Hermia, like two artificial gods,
205 Have with our needles created both one flower,
Both on one sampler, sitting on one cushion,
Both warbling of one song, both in one key,
As if our hands, our sides, voices, and minds,
Had been incorporate. So we grew together,
210 Like to a double cherry—seeming parted

heard your voice, and that's how I found you. Why did
you leave me alone so unkindly?

LYSANDER

Why stay when love tells you to go?

HERMIA

But what love could make my Lysander leave me?

LYSANDER

I had to hurry to my love, beautiful Helena, who lights
up the night better than all those fiery stars. Why are
you looking for me? Didn't you figure out that I left
you because I hate you?

HERMIA

You can't mean what you're saying. It's impossible.

HELENA

So, she's in on this too! Now I see that all three of them
have gotten together to play this cruel trick on me.
Hurtful Hermia, you ungrateful girl, have you conspired with these two to provoke me with this horrible
teasing? Have you forgotten all the talks we've had
together, the vows we made to be like sisters to one
another, all the hours we spent together, wishing that
we never had to say goodbye—have you forgotten?
Our friendship in our schooldays, our childhood
innocence? We used to sit together and sew one flower
with our two needles, sewing it on one piece of cloth,
sitting on the same cushion, singing one song in the
same key, as if our hands, our sides, our voices and our
minds were stuck together. We grew together like
twin cherries—which seemed to be separate but were
also together—two lovely cherries on one stem. We
seemed to have two separate bodies, but we had one
heart. Do you want to destroy our old friendship by

But yet an union in partition—
Two lovely berries molded on one stem;
So, with two seeming bodies but one heart,
Two of the first, like coats in heraldry,
215   Due but to one and crownèd with one crest.
And will you rent our ancient love asunder
To join with men in scorning your poor friend?
It is not friendly, 'tis not maidenly.
Our sex, as well as I, may chide you for it,
220   Though I alone do feel the injury.

HERMIA
I am amazèd at your passionate words.
I scorn you not. It seems that you scorn me.

HELENA
Have you not set Lysander, as in scorn,
To follow me and praise my eyes and face?
225   And made your other love, Demetrius—
Who even but now did spurn me with his foot—
To call me goddess, nymph, divine, and rare,
Precious, celestial? Wherefore speaks he this
To her he hates? And wherefore doth Lysander
230   Deny your love, so rich within his soul,
And tender me, forsooth, affection,
But by your setting on, by your consent?
What though I be not so in grace as you—
So hung upon with love, so fortunate—
235   But miserable most, to love unloved?
This you should pity rather than despise.

HERMIA
I understand not what you mean by this.

HELENA
Ay, do. Persever, counterfeit sad looks,
Make mouths upon me when I turn my back,
240   Wink each at other, hold the sweet jest up—
This sport, well carried, shall be chronicled.
If you have any pity, grace, or manners,

joining these men to insult your poor friend? It's not friendly, and it's not ladylike. All women would be angry with you for doing it, even though I'm the only one who's hurt by it.

HERMIA

I'm completely dumbfounded by what you're saying. I'm not insulting you. It sounds more like you're insulting me.

HELENA

Come on, confess. Didn't you send Lysander, as an insult, to follow me around praising my eyes and my face? Haven't you made your other love, Demetrius—who kicked me with his foot not long ago—call me a goddess and a divine, rare, precious, heavenly creature? Why does he talk like that to a girl he can't stand? And why does Lysander deny that he loves you, when he loves you so deeply? Why would he show me any affection, unless you told him to? Why does it matter that I'm not as lucky or lovable as you are and that the love I feel is unrequited? You should pity me for that reason, not hate me.

HERMIA

I don't know what you're talking about.

HELENA

Oh, fine. All right, go ahead, keep up your little game, pretend to be sympathetic, but then nudge each other and wink and make faces at me when I turn my back. Keep up your wonderful game. You're doing such a good job on this trick, someone should write a book

You would not make me such an argument.
But fare ye well. 'Tis partly my own fault,
245   Which death or absence soon shall remedy.

LYSANDER
Stay, gentle Helena. Hear my excuse.
My love, my life, my soul, fair Helena!

HELENA
Oh, excellent!

HERMIA
(to LYSANDER*)*
                    Sweet, do not scorn her so.

DEMETRIUS
If she cannot entreat, I can compel.

LYSANDER
Thou canst compel no more than she entreat.
250   Thy threats have no more strength than her weak prayers.—
Helen, I love thee. By my life, I do.
I swear by that which I will lose for thee
To prove him false that says I love thee not.

DEMETRIUS
I say I love thee more than he can do.

LYSANDER
255   If thou say so, withdraw and prove it too.

DEMETRIUS
Quick, come.

HERMIA
                    Lysander, whereto tends all this?
(holds LYSANDER *back)*

LYSANDER
(to HERMIA*)*   Away, you Ethiope!

DEMETRIUS
(to HERMIA*)*
                    No, no. He'll

about it. If you had any sense of pity, or manners, you wouldn't pretend to fight over me like this. But goodbye. It's partly my own fault, since I followed you here. Leaving—or dying—will soon take care of everything.

LYSANDER

Stay, lovely Helena. Listen to my excuse. My love, my life, my soul, beautiful Helena!

HELENA

That's a good one.

HERMIA

(to LYSANDER*)* Don't insult her like that, Lysander darling.

DEMETRIUS

(to LYSANDER*)* If Hermia's begging can't make you stop insulting Helena, I can force you to do so.

LYSANDER

You can't force me any more than Hermia can beg me. Your threats are no stronger than her whining.—Helena, I love you. I swear I do. I'll give my life for you, just to prove this guy wrong when he says I don't love you.

DEMETRIUS

I say that I love you more than he does.

LYSANDER

If that's what you say, go fight a duel with me and prove it.

DEMETRIUS

You're on. Let's do it.

HERMIA

Lysander, where are you going with all this?
(she holds LYSANDER *back)*

LYSANDER

(to HERMIA*)* Get away, you African!

DEMETRIUS

(to HERMIA*)* No, no. He'll act like he's going to break

Seem to break loose.
(to LYSANDER*)*

                        Take on as you would follow,
But yet come not. You are a tame man, go!

LYSANDER
(to HERMIA*)* Hang off, thou cat, thou burr! Vile thing, let loose
260   Or I will shake thee from me like a serpent.

HERMIA
Why are you grown so rude? What change is this,
Sweet love?

LYSANDER
                        Thy love? Out, tawny Tartar, out!
Out, loathèd medicine! O hated potion, hence!

HERMIA
Do you not jest?

HELENA
                        Yes, sooth, and so do you.

LYSANDER
265   Demetrius, I will keep my word with thee.

DEMETRIUS
I would I had your bond, for I perceive
A weak bond holds you. I'll not trust your word.

LYSANDER
What, should I hurt her, strike her, kill her dead?
Although I hate her, I'll not harm her so.

HERMIA
(to LYSANDER*)*
270   What, can you do me greater harm than hate?
Hate me? Wherefore? O me! What news, my love?
Am not I Hermia? Are not you Lysander?
I am as fair now as I was erewhile.
Since night you loved me. Yet since night you left me.
275   Why then, you left me—Oh, the gods forbid!—
In earnest, shall I say?

LYSANDER
                        Ay, by my life,

free from you, Hermia. *(to* LYSANDER*)* Pretend like you're going to follow me, but then don't come. You're a coward, get out of here!

LYSANDER

(to HERMIA*)* Stop hanging on me, you cat, you thorn. Let go of me, or I'll shake you off like a snake.

HERMIA

Why have you gotten so rude? What's happened to you, my darling?

LYSANDER

Your darling? Get out, you dark-skinned gypsy! Get out, you horrible poison. Get out!

HERMIA

Are you joking?

HELENA

Of course he is, and so are you.

LYSANDER

Demetrius, I'm ready to fight you as promised.

DEMETRIUS

I wish we had a signed legal contract. I can see you don't keep your promises very well. I don't trust you.

LYSANDER

What? Do you want me to hit Hermia, hurt her, kill her? Sure, I hate her, but I wouldn't hurt her.

HERMIA

(to LYSANDER*)* Can you hurt me any more than by saying you hate me? Hate me? Why? What's happened to you, my love? Am I not Hermia? Aren't you Lysander? I'm as beautiful now as I was a little while ago. You still loved me when we fell asleep, but when you woke up you left me. So you left me—Oh, God help me!—For real?

LYSANDER

I certainly did, and I never wanted to see you again. So stop hoping and wondering what I mean. I've spelled

And never did desire to see thee more.
Therefore be out of hope, of question, of doubt.
Be certain, nothing truer. 'Tis no jest
280   That I do hate thee and love Helena.

HERMIA
O me!
(*to* HELENA) You juggler! You canker-blossom!
You thief of love! What, have you come by night
And stol'n my love's heart from him?

HELENA
                                        Fine, i' faith!
285   Have you no modesty, no maiden shame,
No touch of bashfulness? What, will you tear
Impatient answers from my gentle tongue?
Fie, fie! You counterfeit, you puppet, you!

HERMIA
"Puppet"? Why so?—Ay, that way goes the game.
290   Now I perceive that she hath made compare
Between our statures. She hath urged her height,
And with her personage, her tall personage,
Her height, forsooth, she hath prevailed with him.—
And are you grown so high in his esteem
295   Because I am so dwarfish and so low?
How low am I, thou painted maypole? Speak.
How low am I? I am not yet so low
But that my nails can reach unto thine eyes.

HELENA
(*to* LYSANDER *and* DEMETRIUS)
I pray you, though you mock me, gentlemen,
300   Let her not hurt me. I was never cursed.
I have no gift at all in shrewishness.
I am a right maid for my cowardice.
Let her not strike me. You perhaps may think,
Because she is something lower than myself,
305   That I can match her.

it out for you clearly. It's no joke. I hate you and love
Helena.

HERMIA

Oh, no! *(to HELENA)* You trickster, you snake! You
thief! What, did you sneak in at night and steal my
love's heart from him?

HELENA

Oh, that's very nice! You ought to be ashamed of yourself! You're going to make me mad enough to answer
you? Damn you, you faker, you puppet!

HERMIA

"Puppet"? Why "puppet"?—Oh, I see where this is
going. She's talking about our difference in height.
She's paraded in front of him to show off how tall she
is. She won him over with her height.—Does he have
such a high opinion of you because I'm so short? Is
that it? So how short am I, you painted barber pole?
Tell me. How short am I? I'm not too short to gouge
your eyes out with my fingernails.

HELENA

(to LYSANDER and DEMETRIUS) Please don't let her hurt
me, gentlemen, however much you want to tease me.
I never was much good with insults. I'm not mean and
catty like her. I'm a nice shy girl. Please don't let her
hit me. Maybe you think that because she's shorter
than me I can take her.

HERMIA

                    "Lower"? Hark, again!

HELENA

Good Hermia, do not be so bitter with me.
I evermore did love you, Hermia,
Did ever keep your counsels, never wronged you—
Save that, in love unto Demetrius,
310   I told him of your stealth unto this wood.
He followed you. For love I followed him.
But he hath chid me hence and threatened me
To strike me, spurn me—nay, to kill me too.
And now, so you will let me quiet go,
315   To Athens will I bear my folly back
And follow you no further. Let me go.
You see how simple and how fond I am.

HERMIA

Why, get you gone! Who is 't that hinders you?

HELENA

A foolish heart, that I leave here behind.

HERMIA

320   What, with Lysander?

HELENA

                 With Demetrius.

LYSANDER

Be not afraid. She shall not harm thee, Helena.

DEMETRIUS

(to LYSANDER*)*
No, sir, she shall not, though you take her part.

HELENA

Oh, when she's angry, she is keen and shrewd!
She was a vixen when she went to school.
325   And though she be but little, she is fierce.

HERMIA

"Little" again? Nothing but "low" and "little"!—
Why will you suffer her to flout me thus?
Let me come to her.

HERMIA

"Shorter!" See, she's doing it again!

HELENA

Good Hermia, please don't act so bitter toward me. I always loved you, Hermia, and gave you advice. I never did anything to hurt you—except once, when I told Demetrius that you planned to sneak off into this forest. And I only did that because I loved Demetrius so much. He followed you. And I followed him because I loved him. But he told me to get lost and threatened to hit me, kick me—even kill me. Now just let me go quietly back to Athens. I'll carry my mistakes back with me. I won't follow you anymore. Please let me go. You see how naïve and foolish I've been.

HERMIA

Well, get out of here then! What's keeping you?

HELENA

My stupid heart, which I'm leaving behind here.

HERMIA

What, you're leaving it with Lysander?

HELENA

No, with Demetrius.

LYSANDER

Don't be afraid. She can't hurt you, Helena.

DEMETRIUS

(to LYSANDER) That's right, Hermia won't hurt Helena even if you try to help her.

HELENA

Oh, when you get her angry, she's a good fighter, and vicious too. She was a hellcat in school. And she's fierce, even though she's little.

HERMIA

"Little" again? Nothing but "little" and "short"!— Why are you letting her insult me like this? Let me at her!.

LYSANDER
(to HERMIA*)*   Get you gone, you dwarf,
You minimus of hindering knotgrass made,
330   You bead, you acorn!

DEMETRIUS
                    You are too officious
In her behalf that scorns your services.
Let her alone. Speak not of Helena.
Take not her part. For if thou dost intend
Never so little show of love to her,
335   Thou shalt aby it.

LYSANDER
                    Now she holds me not.
Now follow, if thou darest, to try whose right,
Of thine or mine, is most in Helena.

DEMETRIUS
"Follow"? Nay, I'll go with thee, cheek by jowl.

                    Exeunt LYSANDER *and* DEMETRIUS

HERMIA
You, mistress, all this coil is long of you.
340   Nay, go not back.

HELENA
                    I will not trust you, I,
Nor longer stay in your curst company.
Your hands than mine are quicker for a fray.
My legs are longer though, to run away.

                    Exit HELENA

HERMIA
I am amazed and know not what to say.

                    Exit HERMIA

OBERON
345   *(to* ROBIN*)* This is thy negligence. Still thou mistakest,
Or else committ'st thy knaveries willfully.

LYSANDER

(to HERMIA*)* Get lost, you dwarf, you tiny little weed, you scrap, you acorn!

DEMETRIUS

You're doing too much to defend a woman who wants nothing to do with you. Leave Hermia alone. Don't talk about Helena. Don't take Helena's side. If you continue treating Hermia so badly, you'll pay for it.

LYSANDER

Hermia's not holding onto me anymore. Follow me if you're brave enough, and we'll fight over Helena.

DEMETRIUS

"Follow"? No, I'll walk right next to you, side by side.

DEMETRIUS *and* LYSANDER *exit.*

HERMIA

All this fighting is because of you. Stay where you are.

HELENA

I'm not sticking around here any more. I don't trust you. You might be a better fighter than I am, but my legs are longer and I can run away faster.

HELENA *exits.*

HERMIA

I just can't believe any of this. I don't know what to say.

HERMIA *exits.*

OBERON

(to ROBIN*)* This is all your fault. You make mistakes constantly, or else you cause this kind of trouble on purpose.

ROBIN
Believe me, King of Shadows, I mistook.
Did not you tell me I should know the man
By the Athenian garment he had on?
350 And so far blameless proves my enterprise,
That I have 'nointed an Athenian's eyes.
And so far am I glad it so did sort,
As this their jangling I esteem a sport.

OBERON
Thou seest these lovers seek a place to fight.
355 Hie therefore, Robin, overcast the night.
The starry welkin cover thou anon
With drooping fog as black as Acheron,
And lead these testy rivals so astray
As one come not within another's way.
360 Like to Lysander sometime frame thy tongue,
Then stir Demetrius up with bitter wrong.
And sometime rail thou like Demetrius.
And from each other look thou lead them thus,
Till o'er their brows death-counterfeiting sleep
365 With leaden legs and batty wings doth creep.
(gives ROBIN *another flower)*
Then crush this herb into Lysander's eye,
Whose liquor hath this virtuous property
To take from thence all error with his might
And make his eyeballs roll with wonted sight.
370 When they next wake, all this derision
Shall seem a dream and fruitless vision.
And back to Athens shall the lovers wend,
With league whose date till death shall never end.
Whiles I in this affair do thee employ,
375 I'll to my queen and beg her Indian boy.
And then I will her charmèd eye release
From monster's view, and all things shall be peace.

ROBIN

Believe me, King of Illusions, I made a mistake. Didn't you tell me that I'd be able to recognize the man by the Athenian clothes he was wearing? So far I've done exactly what I was supposed to do—I put the love potion on an Athenian's eyes. And so far I'm pleased with the way things have turned out, since I find all of this commotion very entertaining.

OBERON

As you can see, these lovers are looking for a place to fight. Hurry up, Robin, and make the night dark and cloudy. Cover the sky with a low-hanging fog, as dark as hell, and get these overeager rivals so completely lost in the woods that they can't run into each other. Imitate Lysander's voice and egg Demetrius on with insults. Then rant for a while in Demetrius's voice, and egg Lysander on. That way you'll get them away from each other until they're so exhausted that they'll sleep like the dead. (OBERON *gives a new flower to* ROBIN) When they're asleep, crush some of this flower's juice into Lysander's eyes. The flower's juice has the power to erase all the damage that's been done to his eyes, and to make him see normally, the way he used to. When they wake up, all this trouble and conflict will seem like a dream or a meaningless vision. Then the lovers will go back to Athens, united together until death. While you're busy with that, I'll go see Queen Titania and ask her once again for the Indian boy. And then I'll undo the spell that I cast over her, so she won't be in love with that monster anymore. Then everything will be peaceful again.

ROBIN

My fairy lord, this must be done with haste.
For night's swift dragons cut the clouds full fast,
And yonder shines Aurora's harbinger,
At whose approach, ghosts, wandering here and there,
Troop home to churchyards. Damnèd spirits all,
That in crossways and floods have burial,
Already to their wormy beds are gone.
For fear lest day should look their shames upon,
They willfully themselves exile from light
And must for aye consort with black-browed night.

OBERON

But we are spirits of another sort.
I with the morning's love have oft made sport,
And like a forester the groves may tread
Even till the eastern gate, all fiery red,
Opening on Neptune with fair blessèd beams,
Turns into yellow gold his salt green streams.
But notwithstanding, haste. Make no delay.
We may effect this business yet ere day.

Exit OBERON

ROBIN

Up and down, up and down,
I will lead them up and down.
I am feared in field and town.
Goblin, lead them up and down.
Here comes one.

Enter LYSANDER

LYSANDER

Where art thou, proud Demetrius? Speak thou now.

ROBIN

We've got to act fast, my lord of the fairies. Night's fading quickly, and in the distance the morning star is shining, warning us that dawn is coming. At dawn, the ghosts that have been wandering around all night go home to the graveyards. The souls of people who weren't buried in holy ground, but instead lie rotting by the side of the road or at the bottom of a river, have already gone back to their wormy graves. They weren't buried in a real graveyard because they committed suicide, and they don't want their shame to be seen in daylight, so they avoid sunlight and stay forever in the darkness of night.

OBERON

But we're not like that. We're a different kind of spirit, and we don't have to run away from the sunlight. I like the morning. I often wander around in the woods like a forest ranger until the sun rises in the fiery red sky over the ocean, turning the salty green water to gold. But you should hurry anyway. Don't delay. We still have time to get all of this done before daybreak.

OBERON *exits.*

ROBIN

Up and down, up and down,
I will lead them up and down.
The people fear me in the country and the town.
Goblin, lead them up and down.
Here comes one of them now.

LYSANDER *enters.*

LYSANDER

Where are you, Demetrius, you arrogant bastard? Say something.

ROBIN
(as DEMETRIUS*)*
Here, villain. Drawn and ready. Where art thou?

LYSANDER
I will be with thee straight.

ROBIN
(as DEMETRIUS*)*   Follow me then
To plainer ground.

Exit LYSANDER

Enter DEMETRIUS

DEMETRIUS
Lysander, speak again!
405   Thou runaway, thou coward, art thou fled?
Speak! In some bush? Where dost thou hide thy head?

ROBIN
(as LYSANDER*)* Thou coward, art thou bragging to the stars,
Telling the bushes that thou look'st for wars,
And wilt not come? Come, recreant. Come, thou child!
410   I'll whip thee with a rod. He is defiled
That draws a sword on thee.

DEMETRIUS
Yea, art thou there?

ROBIN
(as LYSANDER*)*
Follow my voice. We'll try no manhood here.

Exeunt

Enter LYSANDER

LYSANDER
He goes before me and still dares me on.
When I come where he calls, then he is gone.
415   The villain is much lighter-heeled than I.
I followed fast, but faster he did fly,

ROBIN

(in DEMETRIUS's voice) I'm over here, you villain, with my sword out and ready to fight. Where are you?

LYSANDER

I'm coming.

ROBIN

(in DEMETRIUS's voice) Let's go to a flatter area where we can fight more easily.

> LYSANDER exits.

DEMETRIUS enters.

DEMETRIUS

Lysander, say something! You coward, did you run away from me? Say something! Are you behind some bush? Where are you hiding?

ROBIN

(in LYSANDER's voice) You coward, are you bragging to the stars and telling the bushes that you want a fight, but then you won't come and fight me? Come here, you coward! Come here, you child! I'll beat you with a stick. It would be shameful to fight you with a sword, the way I would fight with a real man.

DEMETRIUS

Are you there?

ROBIN

(in LYSANDER's voice) Follow my voice. This isn't a good place to fight.

> They exit.

LYSANDER enters.

LYSANDER

He's walking ahead of me, and he keeps daring me to follow him. When I reach the place he's calling from, he disappears. This villain is much quicker than I am. I ran after him fast, but he ran away from me faster, so

That fallen am I in dark uneven way,
And here will rest me.
(lies down)

                              Come, thou gentle day!
For if but once thou show me thy grey light,
420   I'll find Demetrius and revenge this spite.
(sleeps)

Enter ROBIN *and* DEMETRIUS

ROBIN
(as LYSANDER *to* DEMETRIUS*)*
Ho, ho, ho! Coward, why comest thou not?

DEMETRIUS
Abide me, if thou darest! For well I wot
Thou runn'st before me, shifting every place,
And darest not stand nor look me in the face.
425   Where art thou now?

ROBIN
(as LYSANDER*)*   Come hither. I am here.

DEMETRIUS
Nay, then, thou mock'st me. Thou shalt buy this dear
If ever I thy face by daylight see.
Now go thy way. Faintness constraineth me
To measure out my length on this cold bed.
430   By day's approach look to be visited.
(lies down and sleeps)

Enter HELENA

HELENA
O weary night, O long and tedious night,
Abate thy hours. Shine comforts from the east,
That I may back to Athens by daylight
From these that my poor company detest.
435   And sleep, that sometimes shuts up sorrow's eye,
Steal me awhile from mine own company.
(lies down and sleeps)

that now here I am in some dark part of the forest where the ground is uneven. I'll rest here. *(he lies down)* I hope the pleasant daytime comes soon! As soon as the gray light of early morning appears, I'll find Demetrius and get my revenge for this insult.

LYSANDER *lies down and falls asleep.* ROBIN *and* DEMETRIUS *enter.*

ROBIN

(in LYSANDER's *voice)* Ha, ha, ha! Hey, You coward, why aren't you coming?

DEMETRIUS

Wait for me, if you're not too scared! I know that's why you're running away from me, constantly changing places—you're afraid to stand still and wait for me. You're scared to look me in the eye. Where are you now?

ROBIN

(in LYSANDER's *voice)* Come here. I'm over here.

DEMETRIUS

No, you're just taunting me. You'll pay for this if I ever see you face-to-face in the daylight. Go wherever you want. I'm exhausted; I need to lie down and sleep on this cold ground. But watch out. I'll find you at dawn. *(*DEMETRIUS *lies down and sleeps)*

HELENA *enters.*

HELENA

Oh, what a long, tedious, exhausting night! I wish it would end. I wish the comforting light of day would shine so I can go back to Athens and get away from these people who hate me so much. I hope I'll be able to sleep and escape my troubles for a while. People can sometimes forget their difficulties when they're asleep. *(*HELENA *lies down and sleeps)*

ROBIN

Yet but three? Come one more.
Two of both kinds make up four.
Here she comes, cursed and sad.
440   Cupid is a knavish lad
Thus to make poor females mad.

Enter HERMIA

HERMIA

Never so weary, never so in woe,
Bedabbled with the dew and torn with briers,
I can no further crawl, no further go.
445   My legs can keep no pace with my desires.
Here will I rest me till the break of day.
Heavens shield Lysander if they mean a fray!
(lies down and sleeps)

ROBIN

On the ground
Sleep sound.
450   I'll apply
To your eye.
Gentle lover, remedy.
(squeezes flower juice into LYSANDER*'s eyes)*
When thou wakest,
Thou takest
455   True delight
In the sight
Of thy former lady's eye.
And the country proverb known—
That every man should take his own—
460   In your waking shall be shown.
Jack shall have Jill.
Nought shall go ill.
The man shall have his mare again, and all shall be well.
Exit ROBIN

ROBIN

Only three so far? We're still waiting for one more.
Two of both kinds makes four. Ah, here she comes,
angry and sad. Cupid is a bad boy for making poor
women go crazy like this.

HERMIA *enters.*

HERMIA

I've never been more exhausted or upset. I'm all wet
from the dew and scratched up by thorns, and I can't
crawl any farther. I just can't go on. My legs can't hold
themselves up. I'll sleep here until morning. If they do
fight, I hope Lysander is safe! *(*HERMIA *lies down and
sleeps)*

ROBIN

Sleep well there on the ground. I'll cure you, gentle
lover, by putting this medicine on your eyes. *(*ROBIN
puts the nectar of the flower on LYSANDER*'s eyelids)*
When you wake you will be truly delighted to see the
woman you once loved. And when you wake up,
you'll be a walking illustration of the well-known
country proverb. "Jack will have Jill and everything
will be all right."

ROBIN *exits.*

ACT FOUR

SCENE 1

LYSANDER, DEMETRIUS, HELENA, *and* HERMIA *sleep. Enter* TITANIA, *Queen of the Fairies; and* BOTTOM, *with the ass's head; and fairies* PEASEBLOSSOM, COBWEB, MOTH, MUSTARDSEED; OBERON *the king behind them, unseen*

TITANIA
(to BOTTOM*)* Come, sit thee down upon this flowery bed
While I thy amiable cheeks do coy,
And stick musk roses in thy sleek, smooth head,
And kiss thy fair large ears, my gentle joy.

BOTTOM
5   Where's Peaseblossom?

PEASEBLOSSOM
Ready.

BOTTOM
Scratch my head, Peaseblossom. Where's Monsieur
Cobweb?

COBWEB
Ready.

BOTTOM
10   Monsieur Cobweb, good monsieur, get you your weapons
in your hand and kill me a red-hipped humble-bee on the
top of a thistle. And, good monsieur, bring me the honey
bag. Do not fret yourself too much in the action, monsieur.
And good monsieur, have a care the honey bag break not. I
15   would be loath to have you overflown with a honey bag,
signor.

Exit COBWEB

Where's Monsieur Mustardseed?

MUSTARDSEED
Ready.

ACT FOUR

SCENE 1

DEMETRIUS, HELENA, HERMIA, and LYSANDER are still sleeping on the stage. TITANIA *enters with* BOTTOM, *who still has a donkey's head, and the fairies* PEASEBLOSSOM, COBWEB, MOTH, *and* MUSTARDSEED. OBERON *enters behind them, unseen by those onstage.*

TITANIA

(to BOTTOM*)* Come over here and sit down on this flowery bed while I caress those lovable cheeks. I'll put roses on your silky, smooth head and kiss your big, beautiful ears, my gentle darling.

BOTTOM

Where's Peaseblossom?

PEASEBLOSSOM

Here.

BOTTOM

Scratch my head, Peaseblossom. Where's Monsieur Cobweb?

COBWEB

Here.

BOTTOM

Monsieur Cobweb, sir, get out your weapons and kill me a striped bumblebee on a thistle, and bring me its honey. Don't tire yourself out, monsieur. Oh, and monsieur, be careful not to break the honey-sac. I'd hate to see you drowned in honey, sir.

COBWEB exits.

Where's Monsieur Mustardseed?

MUSTARDSEED

Here.

BOTTOM
> Give me your neaf, Monsieur Mustardseed. Pray you,
20   leave your courtesy, good monsieur.

MUSTARDSEED
> What's your will?

BOTTOM
> Nothing, good monsieur, but to help Cavalery Cobweb to
> scratch. I must to the barber's, monsieur, for methinks I am
> marvelous hairy about the face. And I am such a tender ass,
25   if my hair do but tickle me, I must scratch.

TITANIA
> What, wilt thou hear some music, my sweet love?

BOTTOM
> I have a reasonable good ear in music. Let's have the tongs
> and the bones.

TITANIA
> Or say, sweet love, what thou desirest to eat.

BOTTOM
30   Truly, a peck of provender. I could munch your good dry
> oats. Methinks I have a great desire to a bottle of hay. Good
> hay, sweet hay, hath no fellow.

TITANIA
> I have a venturous fairy that shall seek
> The squirrel's hoard and fetch thee new nuts.

BOTTOM
35   I had rather have a handful or two of dried peas. But, I pray
> you, let none of your people stir me. I have an exposition of
> sleep come upon me.

TITANIA
> Sleep thou, and I will wind thee in my arms.
> Fairies, be gone, and be all ways away.

Exeunt FAIRIES

BOTTOM

Give me your first, Mr. Mustardseed. Please, stop bowing, good sir.

MUSTARDSEED

What would you like me to do?

BOTTOM

Nothing, good sir, except to help Sir Cobweb scratch my head. I should go to the barber's, monsieur, because I think I'm getting really hairy around the face. And I'm such a sensitive ass that if my hair even tickles me a little, I need to scratch.

TITANIA

Would you like to hear some music, my sweet love?

BOTTOM

I have a pretty good ear for music. Let's hear someone play the triangle and the sticks.

TITANIA

Or tell me, my sweet love, what you'd like to eat.

BOTTOM

Actually, I'd like a few pounds of grass. I'd like to munch on some good dry oats. Or maybe I've got a hankering for a bundle of hay. There's nothing like good hay, really sweet hay.

TITANIA

I have an adventurous fairy who'll go seek out the squirrel's secret stash and get you some fresh nuts.

BOTTOM

I'd rather have a handful or two of dried peas. But please don't let any of your people wake me up. I really want to sleep now.

TITANIA

Go to sleep, and I will wrap my arms around you. Fairies, go away. Run off in all directions.

The **FAIRIES** *exit.*

40   So doth the woodbine the sweet honeysuckle
      Gently entwist. The female ivy so
      Enrings the barky fingers of the elm.
      Oh, how I love thee! How I dote on thee!

      TITANIA *and* BOTTOM *sleep*
      Enter ROBIN

OBERON
      Welcome, good Robin. Seest thou this sweet sight?
45   Her dotage now I do begin to pity.
      For, meeting her of late behind the wood,
      Seeking sweet favors from this hateful fool,
      I did upbraid her and fall out with her.
      For she his hairy temples then had rounded
50   With a coronet of fresh and fragrant flowers,
      And that same dew, which sometime on the buds
      Was wont to swell like round and orient pearls,
      Stood now within the pretty flowerets' eyes
      Like tears that did their own disgrace bewail.
55   When I had at my pleasure taunted her
      And she in mild terms begged my patience,
      I then did ask of her her changeling child,
      Which straight she gave me and her fairy sent
      To bear him to my bower in Fairyland.
60   And now I have the boy, I will undo
      This hateful imperfection of her eyes.
      And, gentle Puck, take this transformèd scalp
      From off the head of this Athenian swain,
      That, he awaking when the other do,
65   May all to Athens back again repair
      And think no more of this night's accidents
      But as the fierce vexation of a dream.
      But first I will release the fairy queen.
      (squeezing flower juice into TITANIA*'s eyes)*

I'm putting my arms around you just like the woodbine tendril gently twists itself around the sweet honeysuckle, and like the female ivy curls itself around the branches of the elm tree. Oh, how I love you! I'm so crazy about you!

BOTTOM *and* TITANIA *sleep.* ROBIN *enters.*

OBERON

Welcome, good Robin. Do you see this sweet sight? Now I'm starting to pity Titania for being so infatuated. I ran into her recently at the edge of the forest, looking for sweet presents for this hateful idiot, and I scolded her and argued with her. She had put a wreath of fresh, fragrant flowers around his hairy forehead, and the drops of dew that lay in the center of the flowers made the flowers look like they were crying with shame to be decorating the head of that ugly jackass. When I had taunted her as much as I wanted to, and she begged me very nicely to leave her alone, I asked her for the stolen Indian child. She said yes right away, and sent a fairy to bring him to my home in Fairyland. And now that I have the boy, I'll undo the spell that makes her vision so disgustingly wrong. And, gentle Puck, take this transformed ass's head off of the head of that Athenian man, so that when he wakes up at the same time as the rest of them do, they can all go back to Athens. They'll only remember the events of tonight as a very unpleasant dream. But first I'll release the fairy queen from the spell.

(OBERON *squeezes the juice from the second flower into* TITANIA'*s eyes*)

Be as thou wast wont to be.
70   See as thou wast wont to see.
Dian's bud o'er Cupid's flower
Hath such force and blessèd power.
Now, my Titania, wake you, my sweet queen.

TITANIA
(waking) My Oberon, what visions have I seen!
75   Methought I was enamored of an ass.

OBERON
There lies your love.

TITANIA
How came these things to pass?
Oh, how mine eyes do loathe his visage now!

OBERON
Silence awhile.—Robin, take off this head.—
Titania, music call, and strike more dead
80   Than common sleep of all these five the sense.

TITANIA
Music, ho! Music such as charmeth sleep!

Music

ROBIN
(taking the ass's head off BOTTOM*)*
Now when thou wakest, with thine own fool's eyes peep.

OBERON
Sound, music!—Come, my queen, take hands with me,
And rock the ground whereon these sleepers be.
(dances with TITANIA*)*
85   Now thou and I are new in amity,
And will tomorrow midnight solemnly
Dance in Duke Theseus' house triumphantly,
And bless it to all fair prosperity.
There shall the pairs of faithful lovers be
90   Wedded, with Theseus, all in jollity.

Be like you used to be, and see like you used to see.
This bud belongs to Diana, the goddess of virginity,
and it has the power to undo the effects of Cupid's
flower. Now, Titania, wake up, my sweet queen.

TITANIA

(waking up) Oberon, I've had such a strange dream! I
dreamed I was in love with an ass.

OBERON

There's your boyfriend, sleeping right over there.

TITANIA

How did this happen? Oh, I hate looking at his face
now!

OBERON

Be quiet for a while.—Robin, take off his donkey
head.—Titania, get the fairies to play some music,
and make these five people sleep more soundly than
humans have ever slept before.

TITANIA

Music! Play the kind of music that puts people to
sleep.

The music plays.

ROBIN

(removing the ass's head from BOTTOM*)* When you wake
up, see things with your own foolish eyes again.

OBERON

Play the music.—Take my hands, my queen, and
we'll lull these people to sleep with our soft dancing.
(he dances with TITANIA*)* Now that you and I are
friends again, we can dance for Duke Theseus tomorrow at midnight, and bless his marriage and his marriage bed. These other lovers will get married
alongside him, and they'll all be in high spirits.

ROBIN
> Fairy King, attend, and mark.
> I do hear the morning lark.

OBERON
> Then, my queen, in silence sad,
> Trip we after the night's shade.
95
> We the globe can compass soon
> Swifter than the wandering moon.

TITANIA
> Come, my lord, and in our flight
> Tell me how it came this night
> That I sleeping here was found
100
> With these mortals on the ground.

Exeunt OBERON, TITANIA, *and* ROBIN
Wind horn within
Enter THESEUS *and all his train,* EGEUS, *and* HIPPOLYTA

THESEUS
> Go, one of you, find out the forester.
> For now our observation is performed.
> And since we have the vaward of the day,
> My love shall hear the music of my hounds.
105
> Uncouple in the western valley. Let them go.
> Dispatch, I say, and find the forester.

Exit one of the train

> We will, fair queen, up to the mountain's top,
> And mark the musical confusion
> Of hounds and echo in conjunction.

HIPPOLYTA
110
> I was with Hercules and Cadmus once,
> When in a wood of Crete they bayed the bear
> With hounds of Sparta. Never did I hear
> Such gallant chiding. For, besides the groves,

ROBIN

Listen, Fairy King. I can hear the lark singing. Morning's here.

OBERON

In that case, my queen, let's travel silently and solemnly across the globe to where it's still night, circling the earth faster than the moon does.

TITANIA

While we're walking, you can tell me how I ended up sleeping on the ground with these humans last night.

OBERON, TITANIA, *and* ROBIN *exit.*

A hunting horn blows. THESEUS *enters with his servants,* EGEUS *and* HIPPOLYTA.

THESEUS

One of you go find the forest ranger. Since we're done with the May Day rites and it's still so early in the morning, my love will have a chance to hear the beautiful music of my hunting dogs barking as they chase their prey. Unleash the dogs in the western valley. Let them go. Now go find the forest ranger.

A servant exits.

My beautiful queen, we'll go up the mountain and listen to the hounds as their barking echoes in the cliffs and sounds like music.

HIPPOLYTA

I was with the heroes Hercules and Cadmus once, when their Spartan hunting dogs cornered a bear. I'd never heard such impressive barking before. The forests, the skies, the mountains, everything around us

115
The skies, the fountains, every region near
Seemed all one mutual cry. I never heard
So musical a discord, such sweet thunder.

THESEUS
My hounds are bred out of the Spartan kind,
So flewed, so sanded, and their heads are hung
With ears that sweep away the morning dew,
120
Crook-kneed, and dew-lapped like Thessalian bulls,
Slow in pursuit, but matched in mouth like bells,
Each under each. A cry more tunable
Was never hollaed to, nor cheered with horn,
In Crete, in Sparta, nor in Thessaly.
125
Judge when you hear.
(sees the four sleeping lovers)
But, soft! What nymphs are these?

EGEUS
My lord, this is my daughter here asleep.
And this, Lysander. This Demetrius is.
This Helena, old Nedar's Helena.
I wonder of their being here together.

THESEUS
130
No doubt they rose up early to observe
The rite of May, and hearing our intent
Came here in grace our solemnity.
But speak, Egeus. Is not this the day
That Hermia should give answer of her choice?

EGEUS
135
It is, my lord.

THESEUS
Go, bid the huntsmen wake them with their horns.

Exit one of the train

Wind horns and shout within
LYSANDER, **DEMETRIUS**, **HELENA**, *and* **HERMIA** *wake and start up*

seemed to echo the barks of the hounds. I'd never heard such raucous music, such pleasant thunder.

THESEUS

My dogs are bred from Spartan hounds. They have the same folds of flesh around their mouths, the same sandy-colored fur, and hanging ears that brush the morning dew off the grass. They have crooked knees and folds of skin under their necks, just like the Spartan hounds. They're not very fast in the chase, but their barking sounds like bells ringing. Each bark is perfectly in tune with the others, like notes on a scale. No one, anywhere, has ever gone hunting with a more musical pack of dogs. Judge for yourself when you hear them. *(he sees the four lovers sleeping)* But wait a minute! Who are these women?

EGEUS

My lord, that's my daughter asleep on the ground over there, and this is Lysander here, and this is Demetrius, and this is Helena, old Nedar's daughter. I don't understand why they're all here together.

THESEUS

They probably woke up early to celebrate May Day and came here for my celebration when they heard I'd be here. But tell me, Egeus. Isn't today the day when Hermia has to tell us her decision about whether she'll marry Demetrius?

EGEUS

It is, my lord.

THESEUS

Go tell the hunters to blow their horns and wake them up.

A servant exits.

Someone shouts offstage. Horns are blown. LYSANDER, DEMETRIUS, HELENA, *and* HERMIA, *wake up.*

Good morrow, friends. Saint Valentine is past.
Begin these woodbirds but to couple now?

LYSANDER, DEMETRIUS, HELENA, *and* HERMIA *kneel*

LYSANDER
Pardon, my lord.
THESEUS
            I pray you all, stand up.

LYSANDER, DEMETRIUS, HELENA, *and* HERMIA *stand*

(to LYSANDER *and* DEMETRIUS*)*
140 I know you two are rival enemies.
How comes this gentle concord in the world,
That hatred is so far from jealousy
To sleep by hate and fear no enmity?

LYSANDER
My lord, I shall reply amazèdly,
145 Half sleep, half waking. But as yet, I swear,
I cannot truly say how I came here.
But as I think—for truly would I speak,
And now do I bethink me, so it is—
I came with Hermia hither. Our intent
150 Was to be gone from Athens, where we might,
Without the peril of the Athenian law—

EGEUS
(to THESEUS*)* Enough, enough, my lord. You have enough!
I beg the law, the law, upon his head.—
They would have stol'n away, they would, Demetrius,
155 Thereby to have defeated you and me,
You of your wife and me of my consent,
Of my consent that she should be your wife.

DEMETRIUS
(to THESEUS*)* My lord, fair Helen told me of their stealth,
Of this their purpose hither to this wood.

Good morning, my friends. Valentine's Day is over. Are you lovebirds only starting to pair up now?

LYSANDER, DEMETRIUS, HELENA, *and* HERMIA *all kneel.*

LYSANDER

Forgive us, my lord.

THESEUS

Please, all of you, stand up.

LYSANDER, DEMETRIUS, HELENA, *and* HERMIA *get up.*

(to LYSANDER *and* DEMETRIUS*)* I know you two are enemies. Has the world really become so gentle and peaceful that people who hate each other have started to trust each other and sleep beside each other without being afraid?

LYSANDER

My lord, what I say may be a little confused, since I'm half asleep and half awake. I swear, at the moment I really couldn't tell you how I ended up here. But I think—I want to tell you the truth, and now that I think about it, I think this is true—I came here with Hermia. We were planning to leave Athens to escape the Athenian law and—

EGEUS

(to THESEUS*)* Enough, enough, my lord. You've heard enough evidence! I insist that the law punish him— They were going to run away, Demetrius, they were running away to defeat us, robbing you of your wife and me of my fatherly right to decide who my son-in-law will be.

DEMETRIUS

(to THESEUS*)* My lord, the beautiful Helena told me about their secret plan to escape into this forest. I was

160 And I in fury hither followed them,
     Fair Helena in fancy following me.
     But, my good lord, I wot not by what power—
     But by some power it is—my love to Hermia,
     Melted as the snow, seems to me now
165 As the remembrance of an idle gaud
     Which in my childhood I did dote upon.
     And all the faith, the virtue of my heart,
     The object and the pleasure of mine eye,
     Is only Helena. To her, my lord,
170 Was I betrothed ere I saw Hermia.
     But like in sickness did I loathe this food.
     But as in health, come to my natural taste,
     Now I do wish it, love it, long for it,
     And will for evermore be true to it.

THESEUS
175 Fair lovers, you are fortunately met.
     Of this discourse we more will hear anon.—
     Egeus, I will overbear your will.
     For in the temple by and by with us
     These couples shall eternally be knit.—
180 And, for the morning now is something worn,
     Our purposed hunting shall be set aside.
     Away with us to Athens. Three and three,
     We'll hold a feast in great solemnity.
     Come, Hippolyta.

                    Exeunt THESEUS, HIPPOLYTA, EGEUS, *and train*

DEMETRIUS
185 These things seem small and undistinguishable,
     Like far-off mountains turnèd into clouds.

HERMIA
     When everything seems double. Methinks I see these
     things with parted eye,

furious and followed them here, and the lovely Helena
was so in love with me that she followed me. I'm not
sure how it happened—but somehow, something
made my love for Hermia melt away like snow. My
past love for Hermia now seems like a memory of
some cheap toy I used to love as a child. Now the only
person I love, and believe in, and want to look at, is
Helena. I was engaged to her before I ever met Hermia. Then I hated her for a time, as a sick person hates
the food he usually loves. But now I have my natural
taste back, like a sick person when he recovers. Now I
want Helena, I love her, I long for her, and I will
always be true to her.

THESEUS

You pretty lovers are lucky you met me here. We'll
talk more about this later.—Egeus, I'm overriding
your wishes. These couples will be married along with
me and Hippolyta in the temple later today.—And
now, since the morning is almost over, we'll give up on
the idea of hunting. Come with us to Athens. We three
couples will celebrate with a sumptuous feast. Come,
Hippolyta.

THESEUS, HIPPOLYTA, *and* EGEUS *exit
with their followers.*

DEMETRIUS

What exactly just happened? The events of last night
seem small and hard to see clearly, like far-off mountains that look like clouds in the distance.

HERMIA

Yes, it's like my eyes are out of focus, and I'm seeing
everything double.

HELENA
                                        So methinks.
And I have found Demetrius like a jewel,
190 Mine own, and not mine own.

DEMETRIUS
                                        Are you sure
That we are awake? It seems to me
That yet we sleep, we dream. Do not you think
The duke was here, and bid us follow him?

HERMIA
Yea, and my father.

HELENA
                        And Hippolyta.

LYSANDER
195 And he did bid us follow to the temple.

DEMETRIUS
Why then, we are awake. Let's follow him
And by the way let us recount our dreams.

            Exeunt LYSANDER, DEMETRIUS, HELENA, *and* HERMIA

BOTTOM
(waking) When my cue comes, call me, and I will answer.
My next is "Most fair Pyramus." Heigh-ho! Peter Quince?
200. Flute the bellows-mender? Snout the tinker? Starveling?
God's my life, stol'n hence, and left me asleep? I have had
a most rare vision. I have had a dream—past the wit of man
to say what dream it was. Man is but an ass if he go about
to expound this dream. Methought I was—there is no man
205. can tell what. Methought I was, and methought I had—but
man is but a patched fool if he will offer to say what
methought I had. The eye of man hath not heard, the ear of
man hath not seen, man's hand is not able to taste, his
tongue to conceive, nor his heart to report what my dream
210 was. I will get Peter Quince to write a ballad of this dream.

HELENA

Me too. I won Demetrius so easily, as if he were a precious diamond I just found lying around. It's mine because I found it, but I feel like someone else could easily come and claim it was hers.

DEMETRIUS

Are you sure we're awake? It seems to me like we're still sleeping, still dreaming. Do you remember seeing the duke here? Did he tell us to follow him?

HERMIA

Yes, he did. And my father was here too.

HELENA

And Hippolyta.

LYSANDER

And he told us to follow him to the temple.

DEMETRIUS

Well, then, we're awake. Let's follow him. We can tell one another our dreams along the way.

LYSANDER, DEMETRIUS, HELENA, *and* HERMIA *exit.*

BOTTOM

(waking up) Tell me when my cue comes, and I'll say my line. My next cue is "Most handsome Pyramus." Hey! Peter Quince? Flute the bellows-repairman? Snout the handyman? Starveling? My God, they've all run away and left me sleeping here? What a weird dream I had.—You can't even describe such a weird dream. You'd be an ass if you even tried to explain it. I thought I was—no, nobody can even describe what I was. I thought I was, I thought I had—but a person would be an idiot to try to say what I thought I had. No eye has ever heard, no ear has ever seen, no hand has tasted, or tongue felt, or heart described what my dream was like. I'll get Peter Quince to write this

It shall be called "Bottom's Dream" because it hath no bottom. And I will sing it in the latter end of a play before the duke. Peradventure, to make it the more gracious, I shall sing it at her death.

Exit

dream down as a ballad. I'll call it "Bottom's Dream" because it's so deep that it has no bottom. And I'll sing it for the duke in the intermission of a play. Or maybe, to make it even more lovely, I'll sing it when the heroine dies.

BOTTOM *exits.*

ACT 4, SCENE 2

Enter QUINCE, FLUTE, SNOUT, *and* STARVELING

QUINCE
Have you sent to Bottom's house? Is he come home yet?

STARVELING
He cannot be heard of. Out of doubt he is transported.

FLUTE
If he come not, then the play is marred. It goes not forward.
Doth it?

QUINCE
5 It is not possible. You have not a man in all Athens able to
discharge Pyramus but he.

FLUTE
No, he hath simply the best wit of any handicraft man in
Athens.

QUINCE
Yea, and the best person too. And he is a very paramour for
10 a sweet voice.

FLUTE
You must say "paragon." A "paramour" is, God bless us, a
thing of naught.

Enter SNUG

SNUG
Masters, the duke is coming from the temple, and there is
two or three lords and ladies more married. If our sport had
15 gone forward, we had all been made men.

FLUTE
O sweet bully Bottom! Thus hath he lost sixpence a day
during his life. He could not have 'scaped sixpence a day.
An the duke had not given him sixpence a day for playing

ACT 4, SCENE 2

QUINCE, FLUTE, SNOUT, *and* STARVELING *enter.*

QUINCE

Have you sent anyone to Bottom's house? Has he come home yet?

STARVELING

No one's heard from him. I'm sure he's been kidnapped.

FLUTE

If he doesn't show up, the play is ruined. It won't go on. Will it?

QUINCE

No, it would be impossible. He's the only person in Athens who can play Pyramus.

FLUTE

Definitely. He's quite simply the smartest workingman in Athens.

QUINCE

Yes, and the best looking too. And his voice is the paramour of sweetness.

FLUTE

paramour = lover

You mean "paragon." A "paramour" is something bad.

SNUG *enters.*

SNUG

The duke's leaving the temple. Two or three more lords and ladies have been married too. If we'd been able to put on our play, we would have had it made.

FLUTE

Oh that great, funny guy, Bottom! He would have gotten a pension of six pence a day for his whole life. Six pence a day would've been forced on him. I'll be damned if the duke wouldn't have given him six pence

Pyramus, I'll be hanged. He would have deserved it.
20   Sixpence a day in Pyramus, or nothing.

Enter BOTTOM

BOTTOM
    Where are these lads? Where are these hearts?

QUINCE
    Bottom! O most courageous day! O most happy hour!

BOTTOM
    Masters, I am to discourse wonders—but ask me not what,
    for if I tell you I am no true Athenian. I will tell you
25 everything, right as it fell out.

QUINCE
    Let us hear, sweet Bottom.

BOTTOM
    Not a word of me. All that I will tell you is that the duke
    hath dined. Get your apparel together, good strings to your
    beards, new ribbons to your pumps. Meet presently at the
30 palace. Every man look o'er his part. For the short and the
    long is, our play is preferred. In any case, let Thisbe have
    clean linen. And let not him that plays the lion pair his nails,
    for they shall hang out for the lion's claws. And most dear
    actors, eat no onions nor garlic, for we are to utter sweet
35 breath. And I do not doubt but to hear them say, "It is a
    sweet comedy." No more words. Away, go away!

Exeunt

a day for playing Pyramus. And he would have deserved it too. Pyramus is worth six pence a day, or it's worth nothing!

A pension of six pence a day would be a lot of money for a working class man.

BOTTOM *enters.*

BOTTOM

Where are my guys? Where are my good fellows?

QUINCE

Bottom! Oh, how wonderful to see you! Oh, what a relief!

BOTTOM

My friends, I've got some amazing things to tell you—but don't ask me to tell you what. I swear by my Athenian citizenship that I won't tell you anything. I'll tell you everything exactly as it happened.

QUINCE

Tell us, Bottom.

BOTTOM

No, you won't get a word out of me. All I'll tell you is that the duke has had dinner already. Now it's time to get your costumes together. Find some good strings for tying on your false beards, and grab new ribbons to decorate your shoes. Meet me at the palace as soon as possible. Look over your lines again. Our play's going to be performed for the duke! So make sure Thisbe's wearing clean underwear, and make sure whoever's playing the lion doesn't cut his nails, because he needs them long to look like lion's claws. And no one eat any onions or garlic. If we have sweet-smelling breath, I'm sure they'll say "it's a sweet play." Now no more talking. Get busy, go!

They all exit.

ACT FIVE

SCENE 1

Enter THESEUS, HIPPOLYTA, *and* PHILOSTRATE, *with other attendant lords*

HIPPOLYTA
'Tis strange, my Theseus, that these lovers speak of.

THESEUS
More strange than true. I never may believe
These antique fables nor these fairy toys.
Lovers and madmen have such seething brains,
5   Such shaping fantasies, that apprehend
More than cool reason ever comprehends.
The lunatic, the lover, and the poet
Are of imagination all compact.
One sees more devils than vast hell can hold—
10   That is the madman. The lover, all as frantic,
Sees Helen's beauty in a brow of Egypt.
The poet's eye, in fine frenzy rolling,
Doth glance from heaven to Earth, from Earth to heaven.
And as imagination bodies forth
15   The forms of things unknown, the poet's pen
Turns them to shapes and gives to airy nothing
A local habitation and a name.
Such tricks hath strong imagination,
That if it would but apprehend some joy,
20   It comprehends some bringer of that joy.
Or in the night, imagining some fear,
How easy is a bush supposed a bear!

HIPPOLYTA
But all the story of the night told over,
And all their minds transfigured so together,
25   More witnesseth than fancy's images
And grows to something of great constancy,
But, howsoever, strange and admirable.

ACT FIVE
SCENE 1

THESEUS, HIPPOLYTA, *and* PHILOSTRATE *enter, with a number of lords and servants.*

HIPPOLYTA

These lovers are saying some strange things, Theseus.

THESEUS

Yes, strange—and totally made up too. I'll never believe any of these old legends or fairy tales. Lovers and madmen hallucinate about things that sane people just can't understand. Lunatics, lovers, and poets all are ruled by their overactive imaginations. some people think they see devils and monsters everywhere—and they're lunatics. Lovers are just as crazy, and think a dark-skinned gypsy is the most gorgeous woman in the world. Poets are always looking around like they're having a fit, confusing the mundane with the otherworldly, and describing things in their writing that simply don't exist. All these people have such strong imaginations that, when they feel happy, they assume a god or some other supernatural being is bringing that happiness to them. Or if they're afraid of something at night, they look at the shrubbery and imagine it's a wild bear!

HIPPOLYTA

But the story that these lovers are telling, and the fact that they all saw and heard exactly the same things, make me think there's more going on here than imaginary fantasies. Their story is bizarre and astounding, but it's solid and consistent.

Enter lovers: LYSANDER, DEMETRIUS, HELENA, *and* HERMIA

THESEUS
Here come the lovers, full of joy and mirth.—
Joy, gentle friends! Joy and fresh days of love
30   Accompany your hearts!

LYSANDER
                                        More than to us
Wait in your royal walks, your board, your bed!

THESEUS
Come now, what masques, what dances shall we have
To wear away this long age of three hours
Between our after-supper and bedtime?
35   Where is our usual manager of mirth?
What revels are in hand? Is there no play,
To ease the anguish of a torturing hour?
Call Philostrate.

PHILOSTRATE
                                Here, mighty Theseus.

THESEUS
Say, what abridgement have you for this evening?
40   What masque, what music? How shall we beguile
The lazy time if not with some delight?

PHILOSTRATE
(giving THESEUS *a document)*
There is a brief, how many sports are ripe.
Make choice of which your highness will see first.

THESEUS
(reads)
                "The battle with the Centaurs, to be sung
45   By an Athenian eunuch to the harp."
We'll none of that. That have I told my love,
In glory of my kinsman Hercules.
                "The riot of the tipsy Bacchanals,
                Tearing the Thracian singer in their rage."
50   That is an old device, and it was played
When I from Thebes came last a conqueror.

The lovers—LYSANDER, DEMETRIUS, HELENA, *and*
HERMIA—*enter.*

THESEUS

> Here come the lovers, laughing happily.—I wish you
> joy, my friends! I hope the days ahead are full of joy for
> you.

LYSANDER

> We wish you even more joy, and hope joy comes to
> you in your royal walks, at your table, and in your
> royal bed!

THESEUS

> Now, what kind of entertainment do we have to fill up
> the long three hours between dinner and bedtime?
> Where is our entertainment director? What perfor-
> mances have been prepared? Aren't there any plays
> for us to enjoy while we wait in torture for bedtime to
> come? Let me see Philostrate.

PHILOSTRATE

> Here I am, Theseus.

THESEUS

> Tell us what entertainment you've prepared for the
> evening. Which plays, what music? How will we pass
> the time without some entertainment?

PHILOSTRATE

> *(giving* THESEUS *a piece of paper)* Here's a list of all of
> the acts that have been prepared. Choose which one
> you want to see first.

THESEUS

> *(reading)* "The battle between Hercules and the Cen-
> taurs, to be sung by an Athenian eunuch, accompa-
> nied by a harp." No, we won't see that. I've already
> told that story to Hippolyta, while praising my cousin
> Hercules. What else? "The riot of the drunk Baccha-
> nals who rip the singer Orpheus to shreds." That's an
> old show, and I saw it the last time I came back from

    "The thrice three Muses mourning for the death
    Of learning, late deceased in beggary."
  That is some satire, keen and critical,
55 Not sorting with a nuptial ceremony.
    "A tedious brief scene of young Pyramus
    And his love Thisbe. Very tragical mirth."
  "Merry" and "tragical"? "Tedious" and "brief"?
  That is hot ice and wondrous strange snow.
60 How shall we find the concord of this discord?

PHILOSTRATE
  A play there is, my lord, some ten words long,
  Which is as brief as I have known a play.
  But by ten words, my lord, it is too long,
  Which makes it tedious. For in all the play
65 There is not one word apt, one player fitted.
  And tragical, my noble lord, it is.
  For Pyramus therein doth kill himself.
  Which, when I saw rehearsed, I must confess,
  Made mine eyes water—but more merry tears
70 The passion of loud laughter never shed.

THESEUS
  What are they that do play it?

PHILOSTRATE
  Hard-handed men that work in Athens here,
  Which never labored in their minds till now,
  And now have toiled their unbreathed memories
75 With this same play against your nuptial.

THESEUS
  And we will hear it.

PHILOSTRATE
     No, my noble lord.
  It is not for you. I have heard it over,
  And it is nothing, nothing in the world—
  Unless you can find sport in their intents,
80 Extremely stretched and conned with cru 'l pain
  To do you service.

conquering Thebes. "The nine Muses mourning the death of learning and scholarship." That's some sharp, critical satire, and it's not appropriate for a wedding. "A tedious short drama about young Pyramus and his love Thisbe, a very sad and tragic comedy." A sad comedy? Short but still tedious? That's like hot ice and strange snow. How can this drama be so many contradictory things?

PHILOSTRATE

It's a play about ten words long, which is the shortest play I've ever heard of. But in my opinion, it's about ten words too long. That's why it's tedious. In the entire play, not one word is well-written, and not one of the actors is right for his part. It's tragic because Pyramus kills himself. I have to admit that when I saw his suicide during rehearsal, I had tears in my eyes— but they were tears of laughter.

THESEUS

Who are the actors?

PHILOSTRATE

Rough workmen from Athens who never spent much time thinking. Now they've worn out their out-of-shape brains to put on this play for your wedding.

THESEUS

So let's see it.

PHILOSTRATE

No, my noble lord. This play isn't right for you. I've seen the whole thing, and it's completely worthless— unless you think their bad acting and their misremembered lines—which they memorized so painfully—are funny.

THESEUS
                    I will hear that play.
For never anything can be amiss
When simpleness and duty tender it.
Go, bring them in.—And take your places, ladies.

                                    Exit PHILOSTRATE

HIPPOLYTA
85   I love not to see wretchedness o'er charged
And duty in his service perishing.

THESEUS
Why, gentle sweet, you shall see no such thing.

HIPPOLYTA
He says they can do nothing in this kind.

THESEUS
The kinder we, to give them thanks for nothing.
90   Our sport shall be to take what they mistake.
And what poor duty cannot do, noble respect
Takes it in might, not merit.
Where I have come, great clerks have purposèd
To greet me with premeditated welcomes,
95   Where I have seen them shiver and look pale,
Make periods in the midst of sentences,
Throttle their practiced accent in their fears,
And in conclusion dumbly have broke off,
Not paying me a welcome. Trust me, sweet,
100   Out of this silence yet I picked a welcome,
And in the modesty of fearful duty
I read as much as from the rattling tongue
Of saucy and audacious eloquence.
Love, therefore, and tongue-tied simplicity
105   In least speak most, to my capacity.

                    Enter PHILOSTRATE

THESEUS

I'll watch this play. Nothing can really be bad when it's created by simple people who try hard. Come on, bring them in. And sit down, ladies.

PHILOSTRATE exits.

HIPPOLYTA

I don't like seeing poor people overburdened or looking bad when they're trying to do something good.

THESEUS

You won't see anything like that, sweetheart.

HIPPOLYTA

He just said that they're no good at acting.

THESEUS

Then we're even kinder people for thanking them for something that they're not good at. We'll entertain ourselves by accepting their mistakes. When poor dutiful people can't do certain things well, generous people can consider the effort they put into it rather than the effect that they produce. In my travels, great scholars have come up to me, meaning to greet me with well-rehearsed welcoming speeches, and I have seen them tremble and turn pale, and pause inappropriately in the middle of their sentences, and botch their well-rehearsed tones of voice because they're so nervous, and then break off abruptly at the end, without actually welcoming me. Trust me, my sweet, I figured out that they were trying to welcome me even though they were silent, and that message was as clear from someone who was modest and nervously dutiful as it is from someone who is loud and audacious and eloquent. Therefore, love and tongue-tied simplicity can say the most even when they're saying the least, in my opinion.

PHILOSTRATE enters.

PHILOSTRATE

So please your grace, the Prologue is addressed.

THESEUS

Let him approach.

Enter QUINCE *as the* PROLOGUE

PROLOGUE

(delivered by QUINCE*)*
If we offend, it is with our good will.
That you should think we come not to offend,
110   But with good will. To show our simple skill,
That is the true beginning of our end.
Consider then we come but in despite.
We do not come as minding to contest you,
Our true intent is. All for your delight
115   We are not here. That you should here repent you,
The actors are at hand, and by their show
You shall know all that you are like to know.

THESEUS

This fellow doth not stand upon points.

LYSANDER

He hath rid his prologue like a rough colt. He knows not the
120   stop. A good moral, my lord: it is not enough to speak, but
to speak true.

HIPPOLYTA

Indeed he hath played on his prologue like a child on a
recorder—a sound, but not in government.

PHILOSTRATE

Your grace, the person who is going to deliver the prologue is ready.

THESEUS

Let him come forward.

The PROLOGUE (QUINCE) enters.

PROLOGUE

If Quince had read this speech with the proper punctuation, it would mean "If we happen to offend you, we hope you know that we didn't come here intending to offend you, but with the good intention of showing off our little bit of skill. That's all we want to do. Please keep in mind that we came here only to please you. Our true intention is to delight you. We didn't come here to make you sorry. The actors are ready . . ."

If we happen to offend you, it's because we want to. We don't want you to think we came here to offend you, except that we want to offend you with our good intentions. Our plan to show off our little bit of talent will wind up getting us executed. Please keep in mind we're only here out of spite. We don't come here with the intention of making you happy. We're absolutely not here to delight you. The actors are ready to come out and make you sorry. By watching their show, you'll find out everything you're likely to know.

THESEUS

This guy doesn't pay much attention to punctuation.

LYSANDER

He rode that prologue like a wild horse. He didn't know how to stop it. The moral of this story is that it's not enough to speak; you have to speak grammatically.

HIPPOLYTA

Yes, he performed his prologue like a child plays a recorder—he can make sounds, but they're out of control.

THESEUS
His speech was like a tangled chain. Nothing impaired, but
125   all disordered. Who is next?

Enter BOTTOM *as* PYRAMUS,
and FLUTE *as* THISBE,
and SNOUT *as* WALL,
and STARVELING *as* MOONSHINE,
and SNUG *as* LION

PROLOGUE
(delivered by QUINCE*)*
Gentles, perchance you wonder at this show.
But wonder on, till truth make all things plain.
This man is Pyramus, if you would know.
This beauteous lady Thisbe is certain.
130   This man, with lime and roughcast, doth present
Wall, that vile wall which did these lovers sunder.
And through Wall's chink, poor souls, they are content
To whisper. At the which let no man wonder.
This man, with lanthorn, dog, and bush of thorn,
135   Presenteth Moonshine. For, if you will know,
By moonshine did these lovers think no scorn
To meet at Ninus' tomb—there, there to woo.
This grisly beast, which "Lion" hight by name,
The trusty Thisbe, coming first by night,
140   Did scare away, or rather did affright.
And, as she fled, her mantle she did fall,
Which Lion vile with bloody mouth did stain.
Anon comes Pyramus, sweet youth and tall,
And finds his trusty Thisbe's mantle slain.
145   Whereat, with blade, with bloody blameful blade,
He bravely broached his boiling bloody breast.
And Thisbe, tarrying in mulberry shade,
His dagger drew, and died. For all the rest,
Let Lion, Moonshine, Wall, and lovers twain
150   At large discourse, while here they do remain.

THESEUS

His speech was like a tangled chain. It went on and on and was a total mess. Who's next?

BOTTOM *enters as* PYRAMUS, *with* FLUTE *as* THISBE, SNOUT *as* WALL, STARVELING *as* MOONSHINE, *and* SNUG *as* LION.

PROLOGUE

(delivered by QUINCE*)* Ladies and gentlemen, perhaps you are wondering what is going on. Well, keep wondering, until the truth makes everything clear. This man is Pyramus, if you want to know. This beautiful lady is definitely Thisbe. This man with the limestone and cement is portraying Wall, that horrible wall that kept these lovers apart. They are content to whisper through Wall's little hole, the poor souls, and no one should be surprised. This man, with his lantern, dog, and thornbush, portrays Moonshine, because, if you want to know, the lovers were not ashamed to meet each other by moonshine at Ninus's tomb in order to carry on their courtship. This grisly beast, which is called "Lion," scared away, or rather frightened, the faithful Thisbe when she arrived at the meeting place at night. As she ran away from him, she dropped her cloak, which the horrible Lion stained with his bloody mouth. Soon Pyramus comes along, a tall and handsome young man, and finds his faithful Thisbe's cloak to be dead. At this point, he takes his sword, his bloody blameful blade, and bravely breaks open his boiling bloody breast. And Thisbe, hiding in the shade of the mulberry bushes, took his dagger and killed herself. For the rest of the story, let Lion, Moonshine, Wall, and the two lovers talk more about it, since they're standing here.

THESEUS
I wonder if the lion be to speak.

DEMETRIUS
No wonder, my lord. One lion may when many asses do.

Exeunt PROLOGUE, PYRAMUS, THISBE,
LION, *and* MOONSHINE

WALL
(played by SNOUT*)* In this same interlude it doth befall
That I, one Snout by name, present a wall.
155   And such a wall, as I would have you think,
That had in it a crannied hole, or chink,
Through which the lovers, Pyramus and Thisbe,
Did whisper often very secretly.
This loam, this roughcast, and this stone doth show
160   That I am that same wall. The truth is so.
And this the cranny is, right and sinister,
Through which the fearful lovers are to whisper.

THESEUS
Would you desire lime and hair to speak better?

DEMETRIUS
It is the wittiest partition that ever I heard discourse,
165   my lord.

Enter PYRAMUS

THESEUS
Pyramus draws near the wall. Silence!

PYRAMUS
(played by BOTTOM*)*
O grim-looked night! O night with hue so black!
O night, which ever art when day is not!
O night, O night! Alack, alack, alack,

THESEUS

I wonder if the lion's going to talk.

DEMETRIUS

It wouldn't surprise me, my lord. If these asses can speak, a lion should be able to.

PROLOGUE, THISBE, LION, *and* MOONSHINE *exit.*

WALL

(played by SNOUT*)* At this point I, Snout, play a wall. But not just any wall. I want you to understand that I'm pretending to be a kind of wall that has a little hole in it. The lovers Pyramus and Thisbe often whispered very secretly through that hole. This clay, this cement, and this stone that I'm carrying around show that I'm that wall. It's the truth. And this is the crack, right side and left side *(points with two fingers)*, through which the frightened lovers will be whispering.

THESEUS

Can you imagine cement and stone talking better?

DEMETRIUS

It's the smartest partition I've ever heard speak, my lord.

PYRAMUS *enters.*

THESEUS

Pyramus is coming up to the wall. Be quiet!

PYRAMUS

(played by BOTTOM*)* Oh, grim-looking night! Oh, night that is so black in color! Oh night, which is always there when it is not day! Oh night! Oh night! So sad, sad, sad, I'm afraid my Thisbe has forgotten her promise!—And you, oh Wall, oh sweet, oh lovely

170   I fear my Thisbe's promise is forgot!—
        And thou, O Wall, O sweet, O lovely Wall,
        That stand'st between her father's ground and mine.
        Thou Wall, O Wall, O sweet and lovely Wall,
        Show me thy chink to blink through with mine eyne!

        WALL *holds up fingers as chink*

175   Thanks, courteous Wall. Jove shield thee well for this!
        But what see I? No Thisbe do I see.
        O wicked Wall through whom I see no bliss!
        Cursed be thy stones for thus deceiving me!

THESEUS
        The wall, methinks, being sensible, should curse again.

BOTTOM
180   *(out of character)* No, in truth, sir, he should not.
        "Deceiving me" is Thisbe's cue. She is to enter now and I
        am to spy her through the wall. You shall see, it will fall pat
        as I told you. Yonder she comes.

        Enter THISBE

THISBE
        (played by FLUTE*)*
        O Wall, full often hast thou heard my moans,
185   For parting my fair Pyramus and me!
        My cherry lips have often kissed thy stones,
        Thy stones with lime and hair knit up in thee.

PYRAMUS
        I see a voice. Now will I to the chink,
        To spy an I can hear my Thisbe's face. Thisbe?

THISBE
190   My love thou art, my love, I think.

Wall, you stand between her father's property and mine, you Wall, oh Wall, oh sweet and lovely Wall. Show me your hole to stick my eye up against! *(WALL holds up two fingers)* Thank you, you're such a polite wall. God bless you for doing this. But what's this I see? I don't see any Thisbe. Oh wicked wall, through which I don't see any happiness! Damn your stones for disappointing me like this!

THESEUS

Since the wall is conscious, it should curse back at him.

BOTTOM

(out of character) No, actually, sir, he shouldn't say anything. It's not his turn, it's Thisbe's. "Disappointing me like this" is Thisbe's cue. She's supposed to enter now, and I'll see her through the wall. You'll see, it'll happen exactly like I say. Here she comes.

THISBE enters.

THISBE

(played by FLUTE) Oh wall, you've often heard me moaning because you keep me separated from my handsome Pyramus! My cherry lips have often kissed your bricks, which are stuck together with cement.

PYRAMUS

I see a voice! I'll go to the hole to see if I can hear my Thisbe's face. Thisbe?

THISBE

You are my love, my love, I think.

PYRAMUS
> Think what thou wilt, I am thy lover's grace.
> And like Limander am I trusty still.

THISBE
> And I like Helen, till the Fates me kill.

PYRAMUS
> Not Shafalus to Procrus was so true.

THISBE
195   As Shafalus to Procrus, I to you.

PYRAMUS
> Oh, kiss me through the hole of this vile wall!

THISBE
> I kiss the wall's hole, not your lips at all.

PYRAMUS
> Wilt thou at Ninny's tomb meet me straightway?

THISBE
> Tide life, tide death, I come without delay.

Exeunt **PYRAMUS** *and* **THISBE**

WALL
200   Thus have I, Wall, my part dischargèd so.
> And, being done, thus Wall away doth go.

Exit **WALL**

PYRAMUS

I'm your love, no matter what you think. And I'm still faithful to you, just like the famous Limander.

Bottom means the mythical Greek hero Leander, who loved Hero.

THISBE

And I'll be as faithful to you as Helen of Troy, until the day I die.

This is funny not only because Leander loved Hero rather than Helen, but also because Helen was famous for being unfaithful to her husband.

PYRAMUS

Not even Shafalus was as faithful to his lover Procrus as I am to you.

THISBE

Me too, I'm as faithful as Shafalus to Procrus.

They mean to say Cephalus and Procris, two steadfast lovers in Greek mythology.

PYRAMUS

Oh, kiss me through the hole in this nasty wall.

THISBE

But I'm only kissing the wall's hole, not your lips at all.

PYRAMUS

Will you meet me right away at Ninny's grave?

THISBE

Neither death nor life will stop me from coming.

PYRAMUS *and* **THISBE** *exit.*

WALL

I, Wall, have done my part. Now that I'm done, Wall can go away.

WALL *exits.*

THESEUS
Now is the mural down between the two neighbors.

DEMETRIUS
No remedy, my lord, when walls are so willful to hear
without warning.

HIPPOLYTA
205   This is the silliest stuff that ever I heard.

THESEUS
The best in this kind are but shadows, and the worst are no
worse if imagination amend them.

HIPPOLYTA
It must be your imagination then, and not theirs.

THESEUS
If we imagine no worse of them than they of themselves,
210   they may pass for excellent men. Here come two noble
beasts in, a man and a lion.

Enter LION *and* MOONSHINE

LION
(played by SNUG*)*
You, ladies, you whose gentle hearts do fear
The smallest monstrous mouse that creeps on floor,
May now perchance both quake and tremble here,
215   When lion rough in wildest rage doth roar.
Then know that I, as Snug the joiner, am
A lion fell, nor else no lion's dam.
For if I should as lion come in strife
Into this place, 'twere pity on my life.

THESEUS
220   A very gentle beast, of a good conscience.

DEMETRIUS
The very best at a beast, my lord, that e'er I saw.

THESEUS

The lovers should've waited around a little longer—the wall between them is down now.

DEMETRIUS

What can you do? That's what happens with talking walls.

HIPPOLYTA

This is the silliest thing I've ever seen.

THESEUS

The best plays are still only illusions, and the worst are just as good, if you just use your imagination to fill them in.

HIPPOLYTA

In that case it's your imagination that's interesting, not the play.

THESEUS

If we imagine these guys as they imagine themselves, then they're first-class actors. Look, here come two noble animals, a man and a lion.

LION *and* MOONSHINE *enter.*

LION

(played by SNUG*)* You, ladies, whose gentle hearts make you afraid of the smallest monstrous mouse that crawls around on the floor, might quake and tremble now when the wild lion roars in his most violent rage. You should know that I, Snug the carpenter, am not a fierce lion or a lioness, because if I were a lion and I showed up here to cause trouble, I'd be taking my life in my hands.

THESEUS

Ah, it's a sensitive animal, with a good conscience.

DEMETRIUS

He's the best actor I've ever seen play a lion.

LYSANDER
This lion is a very fox, for his valor.

THESEUS
True. And a goose for his discretion.

DEMETRIUS
Not so, my lord. For his valor cannot carry his discretion,
225   and the fox carries the goose.

THESEUS
His discretion, I am sure, cannot carry his valor, for the
goose carries not the fox. It is well. Leave it to his discretion,
and let us listen to the moon.

MOONSHINE
(played by STARVELING*)*
This lanthorn doth the hornèd moon present—

DEMETRIUS
230   He should have worn the horns on his head.

THESEUS
He is no crescent, and his horns are invisible within the
circumference.

MOONSHINE
This lanthorn doth the hornèd moon present.
Myself the man i' th' moon do seem to be—

THESEUS
235   This is the greatest error of all the rest. The man should be
put into the lanthorn. How is it else the "man i' th' moon"?

DEMETRIUS
He dares not come there for the candle. For you see, it is
already in snuff.

HIPPOLYTA
I am aweary of this moon. Would he would change!

THESEUS
240   It appears by his small light of discretion, that he is in the
wane. But yet, in courtesy, in all reason, we must stay the
time.

LYSANDER

He's as brave as a fox.

THESEUS

True. And as wise as a goose.

DEMETRIUS

Oh, that's not true, my lord. He's not brave enough to be wise.

THESEUS

He's not wise enough to be brave. Anyway, he is what he is. Let's listen to the moon.

MOONSHINE

This lantern represents the horned moon—

horned moon = crescent moon

DEMETRIUS

He should have worn the horns on his head.

Cuckolds (husbands whose wives cheat on them) were imagined as having horns.

THESEUS

He's not a crescent moon, so his horns must be invisible inside the circle.

MOONSHINE

This lantern represents the moon. I myself am playing the man in the moon—

THESEUS

Well then, that's the biggest mistake of all. The man should be inside the lantern. How else is he the "man in the moon"?

DEMETRIUS

He can't go in there because of the candle. It's too hot.

HIPPOLYTA

I'm tired of this moon. I wish he'd wax or wane off the stage.

THESEUS

It seems like he's waning, but out of politeness we'll have to wait and see.

LYSANDER
Proceed, Moon.

MOONSHINE
All that I have to say is to tell you that the lanthorn is the
245   moon; I, the man in the moon; this thornbush, my
thornbush; and this dog, my dog.

DEMETRIUS
Why, all these should be in the lanthorn, for all these are in
the moon.—But silence! Here comes Thisbe.

Enter THISBE

THISBE
This is old Ninny's tomb. Where is my love?

LION
250   *(roaring)* Oh!

THISBE *runs off, dropping her mantle*

DEMETRIUS
Well roared, Lion!

THESEUS
Well run, Thisbe!

HIPPOLYTA
Well shone, Moon!—Truly, the moon shines with a good
grace.

LION *bloodies* THISBE*'s mantle*

THESEUS
255   Well moused, Lion!

Enter PYRAMUS

LYSANDER

Go ahead, Moon.

MOONSHINE

All I wanted to tell you is that the lantern is the moon, I'm the man in the moon, this thornbush is my thornbush, and this dog is my dog.

DEMETRIUS

Well, all of these should be in the lantern, because they're all in the moon. But be quiet, here comes Thisbe.

THISBE *enters.*

THISBE

This is old Ninny's tomb. But where is my love?

LION

(roaring) Hey!

THISBE *runs off, dropping her cloak.*

DEMETRIUS

Good roaring, Lion!

THESEUS

Good running, Thisbe!

HIPPOLYTA

Good shining, Moon!—Really, the Moon shines very well.

LION *shakes* THISBE's *cloak around and stains it with blood.*

THESEUS

That's good, Lion! Shake it around like a cat with a mouse.

PYRAMUS *enters.*

DEMETRIUS
    And then came Pyramus.

Exit LION

LYSANDER
    And so the lion vanished.

PYRAMUS
    Sweet Moon, I thank thee for thy sunny beams.
    I thank thee, Moon, for shining now so bright.
260   For by thy gracious, golden, glittering gleams,
    I trust to take of truest Thisbe sight.—
    But stay, O spite!
    But mark, poor knight,
    What dreadful dole is here!
265   Eyes, do you see?
    How can it be?
    O dainty duck! O dear!
    Thy mantle good,
    What, stained with blood?
270   Approach, ye Furies fell!
    O Fates, come, come,
    Cut thread and thrum.
    Quail, crush, conclude, and quell!

THESEUS
    This passion and the death of a dear friend would go near to
275   make a man look sad.

HIPPOLYTA
    Beshrew my heart, but I pity the man.

PYRAMUS
    O wherefore, Nature, didst thou lions frame?
    Since lion vile hath here deflowered my dear,
    Which is—no, no—which was the fairest dame
280   That lived, that loved, that liked, that looked with cheer.
    Come, tears, confound!
    Out, sword, and wound!
    The pap of Pyramus—

DEMETRIUS

And then Pyramus showed up.

LION *exits.*

LYSANDER

So the lion disappeared.

PYRAMUS

Sweet Moon, I thank you for your sunny beams. I thank you, Moon, for shining now so bright, because by the light of your gracious, golden, glittering gleams, I hope to be able to see my faithful Thisbe.—But wait. Oh no! But, look, poor me, what a terrible tragedy is here! Eyes, do you see? How can it be? Oh, dainty duck! Oh, dear! Your cloak so good, what, stained with blood? Come, terrible Furies, and punish whoever has hurt her! Oh, Fate, come and cut the thread of my life. Conquer, crush, conclude, and kill!

THESEUS

You could get sad watching this actor's passionate lament—if one of your good friends happened to die right at the same time.

HIPPOLYTA

Damned if I don't feel sorry for him.

PYRAMUS

Oh, Mother Nature, why did you create lions? A mean and awful lion has deflowered my darling, who is—no, no, who was the most beautiful lady who ever lived, or loved, or liked, or looked. Come on, tears, pour over me! Come on out, sword, and wound Pyra-

Bottom means "devoured," since "deflowered" would mean that the lion had taken Thisbe's virginity.

Ay, that left pap
285   Where heart doth hop. *(stabs himself)*

Thus die I, thus, thus, thus.
Now am I dead.
Now am I fled.
My soul is in the sky.
290   Tongue, lose thy light.
Moon, take thy flight.

Exit MOONSHINE

Now die, die, die, die, die.
(dies)

DEMETRIUS
No die, but an ace for him, for he is but one.

LYSANDER
Less than an ace, man. For he is dead. He is nothing.

THESEUS
295   With the help of a surgeon he might yet recover and prove
an ass.

HIPPOLYTA
How chance Moonshine is gone before Thisbe comes back
and finds her lover?

THESEUS
She will find him by starlight. Here she comes, and her
300   passion ends the play.

Enter THISBE

HIPPOLYTA
Methinks she should not use a long one for such a Pyramus.
I hope she will be brief.

DEMETRIUS
A mote will turn the balance, which Pyramus, which
Thisbe, is the better. He for a man, God warrant us, she for
305   a woman, God bless us.

mus in the chest—yes, right here on the left side where his heart is. (PYRAMUS *stabs himself*)

And so I'm dying. Here I go, here I go. Okay, now I'm dead. My soul has fled to the sky. My tongue shall see no more, It's time for the moon to go away.

MOONSHINE *exits.*

Now die, die, die, die, die. (PYRAMUS *dies*)

DEMETRIUS

Is someone throwing dice? I guess it's "die," not dice, since there's only one of him.

LYSANDER

Actually he's a die with no dots, since he's nothing— he's dead.

THESEUS

With a doctor's help he might recover and become an ass again.

HIPPOLYTA

If Moonshine's gone before Thisbe comes back, how will she be able to see in the dark to find her lover dead?

THESEUS

She'll see him by starlight. Here she comes. Her moaning and groaning will end the play.

THISBE *enters.*

HIPPOLYTA

I don't think a ridiculous Pyramus like that one deserves much moaning. I hope she keeps it short.

DEMETRIUS

I can't decide whether Pyramus or Thisbe is better. God help us if he's a better man. But God help us if she's a better woman.

LYSANDER
She hath spied him already with those sweet eyes.

DEMETRIUS
And thus she means, videlicet—

THISBE
Asleep, my love?
What, dead, my dove?
310   O Pyramus, arise!
Speak, speak. Quite dumb?
Dead, dead? A tomb
Must cover thy sweet eyes.
These lily lips,
315   This cherry nose,
These yellow cowslip cheeks
Are gone, are gone.
Lovers, make moan.
His eyes were green as leeks.
320   O Sisters three,
Come, come to me
With hands as pale as milk.
Lay them in gore,
Since you have shore
325   With shears his thread of silk.
Tongue, not a word.
Come, trusty sword.
Come, blade, my breast imbrue. *(stabs herself)*
And, farewell, friends.
330   Thus Thisbe ends.
Adieu, adieu, adieu.
(dies)

THESEUS
Moonshine and Lion are left to bury the dead.

DEMETRIUS
Ay, and Wall too.

LYSANDER

Look, she's spotted him with those sweet eyes of hers.

DEMETRIUS

And now she'll start moaning, of course—

THISBE

Are you asleep, my love? What, are you dead, my dove? Oh, Pyramus, get up! Speak, speak. Can't you talk? Dead, dead? The dirt of a grave must cover your sweet eyes! Your lily-white lips, your cherry-red nose, and your buttercup-yellow cheeks are gone, gone forever. Lovers, moan and weep. His eyes were as green as leeks. Oh, Fate, come, come to me, with hands as pale as milk. Soak your hands in blood and gore, since you have cut the thread of his life with scissors. Tongue, do not speak. Come, trusty sword. Come, blade, drench my breast with blood. *(she stabs herself)* Goodbye, friends! This is how Thisbe comes to an end. Goodbye, goodbye, goodbye. (THISBE *dies)*

THESEUS

Moonshine and Lion are left to bury the dead.

DEMETRIUS

Yes, and Wall too.

BOTTOM
(out of character) No, assure you. The wall is down that
335   parted their fathers. Will it please you to see the epilogue,
or to hear a Bergomask dance between two of our company?

THESEUS
No epilogue, I pray you, for your play needs no excuse. Never
excuse—for when the players are all dead, there needs none
to be blamed. Marry, if he that writ it had played Pyramus
335   and hanged himself in Thisbe's garter, it would have been a
fine tragedy. And so it is, truly, and very notably discharged.
But come, your Bergomask. Let your epilogue alone.

Bergomask dance

Exeunt BOTTOM *and* FLUTE

The iron tongue of midnight hath told twelve.
Lovers, to bed. 'Tis almost fairy time.
345   I fear we shall outsleep the coming morn
As much as we this night have overwatched.
This palpable-gross play hath well beguiled
The heavy gait of night. Sweet friends, to bed.
A fortnight hold we this solemnity,
350   In nightly revels and new jollity.

Exeunt

Enter ROBIN

ROBIN
Now the hungry lion roars
And the wolf behowls the moon,
Whilst the heavy ploughman snores,
All with weary task fordone.
355   Now the wasted brands do glow,
Whilst the screech-owl, screeching loud,
Puts the wretch that lies in woe
In remembrance of a shroud.
Now it is the time of night
360   That the graves all gaping wide,

BOTTOM

(out of character) No, I assure you. The wall that kept their fathers apart has been taken down. Would you like to see the epilogue or hear a country dance between two of us?

THESEUS

No epilogue, please. Your play doesn't need to be excused afterward with an epilogue. Never apologize—when the actors are all dead, no one can be blamed. As a matter of fact, if the playwright had played Pyramus and hanged himself with Thisbe's belt, it would have been a very good tragedy. It's a good tragedy, very well done. But come on, let's see you do your dance. Forget your epilogue.

The actors dance, and **BOTTOM** *and* **FLUTE** *exit.*

The clock has chimed midnight. Lovers, it's time to go to bed. It's almost fairy time. I'm afraid we're going to oversleep in the morning as late as we've stayed up tonight. This blatantly stupid play helped us kill the time until bed. Dear friends, let's go to bed. We'll continue this celebration for two weeks, with nightly parties and new fun.

They all exit.

ROBIN *enters.*

ROBIN

Now the hungry lion roars and the wolf howls at the moon. The farmer snores, exhausted from his work. The charred logs glow in the fireplace, and the owl's hoot makes the sick man think about his own death. Now is the time of night when graves open wide and release spirits to glide over the graveyard paths. And we fairies, who run away from the sun just like the

> Every one lets forth his sprite,
> In the churchway paths to glide.
> And we fairies, that do run
> By the triple Hecate's team
365 > From the presence of the sun,
> Following darkness like a dream,
> Now are frolic. Not a mouse
> Shall disturb this hallowed house.
> I am sent with broom before
370 > To sweep the dust behind the door.

Enter OBERON *and* TITANIA, *King and Queen of Fairies, with all their train*

OBERON

> Through the house give glimmering light,
> By the dead and drowsy fire.
> Every elf and fairy sprite
> Hop as light as bird from brier.
375 > And this ditty, after me,
> Sing and dance it trippingly.

TITANIA

> First, rehearse your song by rote,
> To each word a warbling note.
> Hand in hand with fairy grace
380 > Will we sing and bless this place.

OBERON, TITANIA, *and the* FAIRIES *sing and dance*

OBERON
(sings)

> *Now until the break of day,*
> *Through this house each fairy stray.*
> *To the best bride bed will we,*
> *Which by us shall blessèd be.*
385 > *And the issue there create*
> *Ever shall be fortunate.*
> *So shall all the couples three*

goddess of the night, following darkness like a dream,
are getting antsy. But I'm here to make sure that not
even a mouse disturbs this blessed house. I've been
sent to clean house a bit before the fairies come.

OBERON *and* TITANIA *enter with their servants and
followers.*

OBERON

Let the dying fire shine a glimmering light throughout
the house. I want every elf and fairy to hop lightly, like
a bird on a twig, and to sing and dance this song along
with me.

TITANIA

First rehearse your song from memory, and make sure
each note is pretty. We'll all join hands and sing, and
bless this place with our fairy grace.

OBERON *and* TITANIA *lead the* FAIRIES *in song and
dance.*

OBERON

(singing)

> *Now, until morning, each fairy should walk
> through this house. Titania and I will go to the
> royal marriage bed to bless it, and the children
> conceived in that bed will always have good luck.
> Each of the three couples will always be faithful
> and in love, and their children will have no*

Ever true in loving be.
And the blots of Nature's hand
390 *Shall not in their issue stand.*
Never mole, harelip, nor scar,
Nor mark prodigious, such as are
Despisèd in nativity,
Shall upon their children be.
395 *With this field dew consecrate,*
Every fairy take his gait.
And each several chamber bless
Through this palace with sweet peace.
And the owner of it blessed
400 *Ever shall in safety rest.*
Trip away. Make no stay.
Meet me all by break of day.

Exeunt all but ROBIN

ROBIN

If we shadows have offended,
Think but this, and all is mended—
405 That you have but slumbered here
While these visions did appear.
And this weak and idle theme,
No more yielding but a dream,
Gentles, do not reprehend.
410 If you pardon, we will mend.
And, as I am an honest Puck,
If we have unearnèd luck
Now to 'scape the serpent's tongue,
We will make amends ere long.
415 Else the Puck a liar call.
So good night unto you all.
Give me your hands if we be friends,
And Robin shall restore amends.

Exit

deformities. *They won't have moles, or harelips, or scars, or abnormal markings, or anything else that might alarm someone if their baby was born with it. Use this blessed dew from the fields to bless each room in the palace with sweet peace. And the blessed owner will always be safe. Run along. Don't stay long. Meet me at dawn.*

They all exit except for ROBIN.

ROBIN

If we actors have offended you, just think of it this way and everything will be all right—you were asleep when you saw these visions, and this silly and pathetic story was no more real than a dream. Ladies and gentlemen, don't get upset with me. If you forgive us, we'll make everything all right. I'm an honest Puck, and I swear that if we're lucky enough not to get hissed at, we'll make it up to you soon. If not, then I'm a liar. So good night to everyone. Give me some applause, if we're friends, and Robin will make everything up to you.

He exits.

SPARKNOTES LITERATURE GUIDES